Making a Difference

For Agnes and Ed Marquette
with admiration
and gratitude for
your friendship
and help.

Whitney North Seymour Jr

March 1984

Books by Whitney North Seymour, Jr.

Making a Difference

BY

Whitney North Seymour, Jr.

William Morrow and Company, Inc.
New York 1984

Grateful acknowledgment is made for permission to reprint lines from "The Road Not Taken" from *The Poetry of Robert Frost* edited by Edward Connery Lathem. Copyright 1916 by Holt, Rinehart & Winston. Copyright 1944 by Robert Frost. Reprinted by permission of Holt, Rinehart & Winston, publishers.

Library of Congress Cataloging in Publication Data

Seymour, Whitney North, 1923–
  Making a difference.

  Bibliography: p.
  Includes index.
  1. Conduct of life. 2. United States—Biography.
I. Title.
BJ1581.2.S46 1984   170'.44   83-19416
ISBN 0-688-02652-4

Printed in the United States of America

First Edition

1 2 3 4 5 6 7 8 9 10

BOOK DESIGN BY PATTY LOWY

For Catryna, who has made a
tremendous difference in all
of our lives

Acknowledgments

The idea for this work grew out of conversations with Elizabeth N. Layne while we were working together on an earlier book urging affirmative action to save the nation's public libraries (*For the People, Fighting for Public Libraries,* Doubleday, 1979). As we discussed the many good-hearted people who render unselfish public service for libraries, we wondered why so many other people, who have every advantage, never seem to lift a finger to help their communities or their fellow man. Soon we found ourselves making up lists of the people we admired for their commitment to public service, and trying to find the common factors that motivated and sustained them.

We began talking about sharing what we learned with others and came to believe that people who are disappointed with their lives would welcome a chance to study examples of how others had achieved rich and satisfying careers through unselfish service to others. Soon the book had begun. Liz continued to play a major role in the basic research for the book and has patiently reviewed and critiqued the preliminary drafts. Her imprint is everywhere in the final product.

The other major forces that shaped this book were

the members of my family—Catryna, Tryntje and Gabriel. They shared the discovery of character strengths and weaknesses of folk heroes we all admire. We pondered together the qualities that separate good people from selfish, accomplishment from avarice, sincere generosity from disguised greed. They looked over drafts of various chapters and offered affirmative suggestions, and, more important, they offered encouragement. The final product is a family effort in every sense.

I must also acknowledge my personal indebtedness to the people whose own examples inspired me to believe in the ideal of public service, principal among whom have been my late father, Whitney North Seymour, who brought out the best in everyone through unceasing kindness; J. Edward Lumbard, the first U.S. Attorney under whom I served, a true exponent of the public service ideal; and Orison S. Marden, president of the New York City, New York State, and American bars, who exercised leadership through gentle, steadfast support of high principles and worthwhile goals. Great men all.

I especially want to acknowledge the reinvigoration of spirit provided by young people with whom I served in the U.S. Attorney's Office for the Southern District of New York. Over the years they have demonstrated a commitment to public service which has proven again and again that practical idealism can overcome cynicism and greed.

—WHITNEY NORTH SEYMOUR, JR.
New York, July 1983

Contents

10   *Contents*

Two roads diverged in a wood, and I—
I took the one less traveled by,
And that has made all the difference.

—ROBERT FROST
The Road Not Taken

Introduction

I wish that there were some wonderful place
Called the Land of Beginning Again,
Where all our mistakes and all our heartaches
And all of our poor selfish grief
Could be dropped like a shabby old coat at the door,
And never be put on again.

—Louisa Fletcher,
from *Best Loved Poems of
the American People*

We live in The Age of Cynicism. People who think of themselves as sophisticates enjoy puncturing other people's dreams. They compete for cleverness in leveling everything and everybody. They give priority to financial rewards, titles and position.

Why?

Who will miss them when they are gone—their stockbrokers?

When they look back over their achievements in their old age, what will they see—a comfortable net worth?

13

Is that what life is about? The biblical injunction "Lay not up for yourselves treasures upon earth ... but lay up for yourselves treasures in heaven" is based on real-life experience. Human happiness comes not from a fat portfolio but from love, from sharing, from serving others.

Economic independence is obviously a necessity for all human beings. But once security is achieved, there can be no justification for seeking more and more.

Greed is the social sickness of our time, worse than any black plague in history. It breeds dishonesty, distrust, envy—all the things that make life ugly.

There will always be some people who see everything as hopeless and everyone as out only for personal gain. These are the same people whose first question is: "What's in it for me?"

What future is there for our planet? The spectre of nuclear warfare makes everything academic. Our society is sick; all politicians are dishonest; our children have nothing to look forward to. Why bother?

"Vote your hopes, not your fears" was the response of Norman Thomas to people who told him they admired him personally but would not vote for him for fear they might help elect the candidate they liked the least by casting their vote where it would not affect the election outcome.

"*Live* your hopes, not your fears" is the message of this book. The planet will not be saved unless we help to save it. Society's ills will not be cured unless we help to cure them.

Morality requires much more than writing Letters to the Editor and making tax-deductible contributions.

It requires a commitment to honesty, decency, sincerity, humility.

In our era of high technology and corporate-tender offers, the ideal of service to others has been almost entirely replaced by the idol of wealth and economic success. More young people want to become doctors to get rich than to heal the sick. More want to become lawyers to handle big corporate deals than to help the underdog. In almost any field you can name, the things people seem to want most are power, wealth and status.

A few years ago, Louis Kronenberger wrote a lament in *Horizon* magazine, entitled "Whatever Became of Personal Ethics?" Mr. Kronenberger's theme was that achievers in present-day America possess split personalities—they give lip service and a few dollars to worthy causes, while engaging in malicious and unethical conduct in their own careers:

> They can help their fellow man wherever he is segregated or jailed or flogged, censored or silenced, slum-dwelling or dispossessed. They only cannot when he is their colleague or competitor, their friend or peer. And this seems new to me—a dog-eat-dog careerism that crusades for the underdog. These people do steadily, quite early in life, what the hard-fisted rich used to do very late: *they pay conscience money.* But today's, unlike yesterday's, is not paid retroactively in leisured remorse; it is pay-as-you-go penance.

Mr. Kronenberger warned that among many intelligent, educated people, *social* morality has been substituted for *personal* morality:

> How ultimately great is the gain to bring up children with no prejudice against race and with every sympathy for the poor, if they are to have no scruples

against back-stabbing, and an utter apathy toward fair play?

A recent magazine ad for an after-dinner drink uses a quotation from Gerald Murphy, a member of Gertrude Stein's "lost generation":

Living well is the best revenge.

Revenge for what? Against whom? Revenge against the courageous colonials who gathered in Philadelphia two hundred years ago and put their lives, their property, their families, their worldly possessions on the line by signing the Declaration of Independence?

Revenge against the citizen soldiers who, over the course of two centuries, have risked battle wounds or death to ensure our enjoyment of "life, liberty and the pursuit of happiness"?

The title of this book refers to that pursuit of happiness—not for material possessions and creature comforts, but for an inner sense of fulfillment: the knowledge that we have done the best we possibly can to help others and to make the world a better place than we found it. The title is taken from the final line of Robert Frost's poem *"The Road Not Taken"*—it is the result of choosing the road "less traveled by."

Supreme Court Justice Louis D. Brandeis said that the great happiness in life is "not to *donate* but to *serve."* It is about service that this book is written.

The difference is service, not charity. Giving our most precious possession—part of our lives—to helping others.

The difference may be direct help to those in need; combating injustice, corruption, dishonesty; creating and preserving beauty—manmade as well as natural; generosity toward friends, acquaintances, neighbors, strangers; assisting others in achieving and enjoying economic freedom, and freedom of mind and spirit.

The difference for most people can be achieved as a second vocation, fitted in alongside the practical demands of supporting self and dependents. Where it is possible to commit full time (as in retirement), service need not be so time-consuming that it produces self-pity and resentment. It must truly be the pursuit of *happiness.*

The difference is humility and kindness in human relations, and in relations with nature and nature's creatures. It is the unexpected smile; treating all persons with equal respect and dignity; taking a sincere interest in the concerns and pleasures of others; praising achievement; rewarding effort.

This is not a how-to-succeed book in the conventional sense. It is a guide to a life where helping others is more important than wealth or position. It is a book about doing good rather than about doing well. It seeks to inspire by example.

Above all, it is an appeal for affirmative action to strive to make the world a better place.

Developing Personal Discipline

Be Independent

Behold the turtle, he makes progress only when he
sticks his neck out.

> *—Sign on the office wall of James B. Conant,*
> *President of Harvard University*

To many of his contemporaries Henry David Thoreau
was a "nut." Today we recognize him as one of
America's truly independent thinkers who had the
courage to defy convention and, as a result, made significant contributions to world morality.

Thoreau was a mild-mannered writer-naturalist
when he made up his mind not to pay his poll tax. The
tax proceeds were to help pay for the costs of the Mexi-
can War, and Thoreau was convinced that the war
would produce an extension of slavery to the South-
west. He was strongly opposed to slavery and to the
war, and refusal to pay the tax seemed to him the best
way to state his opposition forcefully. The tax collector
had him locked up overnight in the town jail.

After his jail stay, Thoreau published an essay,
"On the Duty of Civil Disobedience," which appeared
in 1849. In it he argued that individual citizens have a

responsibility of passive resistance to government actions they consider unjust. Thoreau's doctrine later became the basis for the civil rights movement in the United States in the 1950s and 1960s. It found adherents in other parts of the world as well, most notably in the resistance movement led by Mahatma Gandhi against British rule in India.

Thoreau himself was a surprisingly quiet-spoken person for one whose writings seem so inflammatory. He grew up on a small farm near Concord, enrolled in Harvard College at the age of sixteen, studied Latin, Greek and the English classics, and stood near the top of his class. He became a schoolteacher and lecturer. Fascinated by the transcendentalist writings of his neighbor Ralph Waldo Emerson, he decided to test for himself the relationship of man and nature.

In 1841, he set down his plan in his journal: He would go to live by the edge of a pond, "Where I shall hear only the wind whispering among the reeds. It will be a success if I have left myself behind."

Emerson offered to let Thoreau build a cabin on his land near Walden Pond outside Concord, in return for clearing a patch of briars and planting the area with pines. For two years Thoreau conducted his one-man revolution in this natural habitat, living as simply as possible (his food, in addition to what he gathered or grew, cost him only twenty-seven cents a week). He spent long hours every day studying nature and writing his observations in his journal.

Thoreau's biographer, H. S. Canby, described Thoreau's experience as a test of self-reliance:

> His plan went no further than to find a way in which a poor scholar, who was a skilful handyman,

could live in independence with time enough to do what he wanted, and a wide margin of leisure in which to reflect and enjoy. His intent was, first to make a satisfactory life for himself, and, next, to go on with his reporting of experience for his contemporaries. But the result was a challenge to his neighbors that became a challenge to a rapidly industrializing world—a challenge to each individual in any race, under any circumstance, to discover, as the Hindu said, his own peculiar genius, and, having learned what he wanted to do, to learn how to do what he wanted.

After two years of living under extremely simple conditions, Thoreau returned to "civilization" and began to write about his experiences for publication, to share them with the world.

He urged his readers to "simplify, simplify." To break the bonds of conventional opinion, of things, money, fame, respectability:

> Decide first how much time you care to give to earning your living and set your standard of life accordingly [he advised]. Before you try to keep up with the Joneses you should first find out where the Joneses are going and whether that is a desirable direction for you.

Thoreau scorned those whose lives are fueled by material things:

> Many a poor immortal soul have I met well-nigh crushed and smothered under its load, creeping down the road of life, pushing before it a barn ... and one hundred acres of land, tillage, mowing, pasture and woodlot.

Only by eliminating the pressures of possessions could the individual be truly independent, he said.

Thoreau was one of the earliest conservation activists, decrying the destruction of landscapes and wildlife, and urging young people to live in close harmony with nature. Although he died of tuberculosis at the age of forty-five, his staunch independence has continued to inspire hundreds of thousands of people to resist the encroachments of industrialization.

Thoreau's contemporaries poked fun at his eccentricities. Some accused him of putting on a pose to get attention; others of engaging in bravado. The criticism, of course, only added to the tenacity of Thoreau's independence. Today it serves as fair warning that anyone who strikes out on an independent course must be ready to take in stride the ridicule which surely will follow. The rewards must come from within.

More than a decade before Thoreau's well-publicized act of civil disobedience, America had witnessed an even more dramatic example of personal independence by a young Connecticut woman, whose actions helped to galvanize the early movement to abolish slavery.

Prudence Crandall, mild-mannered daughter of a Quaker farm couple, was twenty-eight when a committee of leading citizens of Canterbury, Connecticut, invited her to establish a genteel school for young ladies in one of the fine houses on the town green. The Canterbury Female Boarding School soon was flourishing. Then one day, the headmistress admitted to the student body a seventeen-year-old black girl, daughter of a successful local farmer, who wanted to study to become a teacher. The leading citizens met with Miss Crandall and attempted to persuade her to reverse her decision and turn the new student out. When persuasion did not work, they threatened to cut off financial support and to withdraw the other students.

Prudence Crandall, outraged at the intolerance of the community, decided on a direct course of action. She closed the school.

Then, after conferring in Boston with William Lloyd Garrison, a leader of the fledgling abolitionist movement and a supporter of equal education for free blacks, Prudence Crandall reopened her Canterbury school as a teacher-training academy for Negro girls. She recruited the daughters of affluent black families in Boston, Providence and New York.

The town fathers retaliated. Merchants refused to supply the school with food. Students were barred from attending services at the Congregational Church. Threats were made to arrest the youngsters as paupers and vagrants. Stones and rotten eggs were hurled at the school; mud was smeared on the front steps; manure was thrown down the well. Despite it all, Prudence Crandall went on teaching her students, somehow managing to sidestep the impediments thrown in her way.

The full power of state government was brought to bear on the young woman who so obstinately insisted on educating black children. The Connecticut state legislature outlawed all schools that taught out-of-state blacks and authorized town officials to ban the teaching of "any colored person" who was not a permanent resident of the town.

Prudence Crandall was arrested for violating the new state law. She spent her first night in a cell recently occupied by a convicted murderer. After her release on bail, she was brought to trial on two separate occasions and was finally discharged only after an appeals court discovered a technical defect in the indictment.

The citizens of Canterbury once again turned to vigilante actions. Unidentified persons tried to set the school building on fire. When this failed, a group of men advanced on the school with iron bars and smashed every window in the building. Fearing that increasing mob violence would result in injury to her students, Prudence Crandall reluctantly at last closed the school and moved away.* For almost two years she had stood her ground. Abolitionist newspapers spread the story of the lone woman's independent fight against bigotry, and more and more people began to join the cause.

When Hannah Stone gave birth to her eighth child, Lucy, she said wistfully, "Oh, dear! I am sorry it is a girl. A woman's life is so hard."

Mrs. Stone knew. Just before she went into labor, she had gone to the barn to milk the family's herd of eight cows. The year was 1818.

Throughout her childhood, Lucy did household chores on the family farm in eastern Massachusetts. In the mornings, before the sun was up, she drove the cows out to pasture. She churned butter; she cooked; she helped with the laundry.

Lucy increasingly resented the disparity in status between men and women. Men owned the family prop-

---

* Her plans were to open another school in one of the larger Eastern cities, but the failing health of her new husband forced a move to Illinois, where she established a small school in her own home. Fifty years later, the Connecticut legislature attempted to make amends by voting her a small annuity during her final years.

erty. Men earned higher wages for the same work. Men went to college.

While still quite young, Lucy joined the Congregational Church. One day she attended a meeting of the congregation to hear the case against Deacon Henshaw, whose antislavery sentiments had resulted in charges of unbecoming conduct. After the case was presented and the deacon's fate was put to a vote, Lucy, not knowing the church forbade women the vote, raised her hand and heard the minister instruct a teller, "Don't count her. She is not a voting member."

Lucy Stone recalled the incident vividly many years later:

> That afternoon they took six other votes, and every time I held my hand up high; every time they did not count it. All the same I held my hand up.

Independence had taken firm root in the gentle, free spirit of Lucy Stone. She longed for an education—a real one, like the college training her brothers were receiving with her father's help. But her father would hear none of it.

When she was seventeen, Lucy and a group of her friends decided to seek permission to attend lectures at nearby Harvard College in Cambridge. They paid a call on President Quincy, who first tried to dissuade them by logic, then finally declared, "The time will never come when Harvard will open its doors to women."

Quincy's arrogance fired Lucy's determination. She started working at odd jobs and saving the pennies she earned. She sold berries in summer and chestnuts in winter and used the money to buy books. At nineteen she began to teach school. The experience increased her determination to be independent. When she was called to be a substitute teacher for one of her brothers for several weeks, she was paid sixteen dollars a month for the same work for which he had received thirty dollars, because "that was enough for a woman."

By the age of twenty-five, Lucy Stone had scraped and saved enough to go to college on her own. Oberlin College in Ohio was the only institution which then admitted women. She traveled across Lake Erie by "deck passage," along with horses and freight, to reach Cleveland from Buffalo. At Oberlin she worked in the Ladies' Boarding Hall for three cents an hour to earn her keep, and taught in the college's preparatory school to pay her other expenses. Years later her father would say to her, "You were right and I was wrong." But at the time there was no financial help from home, and Lucy could not return home for holidays or vacations.

In 1847, Lucy Stone graduated from Oberlin College with honors, and became the first Massachusetts woman to earn a college degree.

But when she was asked to prepare a talk for the graduation ceremony to be read by one of the male faculty members (since it was not proper for a woman to read in public), she declined.*

Before she went off to college, Lucy Stone remembered hearing the reading of the "Pastoral Letter" which criticized the Grimké sisters for speaking publicly against slavery (see Chapter 9). The clergy had condemned public speaking by women as a "danger

* Decades later she was invited to be a featured speaker at Oberlin's semi-centennial celebration.

which threatened the female character with wide-spread and permanent injury." As Lucy Stone listened to the "Letter," she became more and more incensed:

> My indignation blazed and I told my cousin that, if I ever had anything to say in public, I should say it, and all the more because of that "Pastoral Letter"!

Now she was to have her chance. One of her brothers, the Reverend William B. Stone, invited her to speak from his pulpit in Gardner, Massachusetts, about women's rights. The news spread. Soon afterward, she was invited to speak on behalf of the Anti-Slavery Society at the town hall in Malden. A local minister announced the lecture to his congregation as follows:

> I am requested by Mr. Mowry to say that a hen will undertake to crow like a cock at the Town Hall this afternoon at five o'clock.

This rudeness brought out a huge crowd to hear Lucy Stone. Soon she was traveling a lecture circuit around the United States. Her message was always the same—abolish slavery and give women the vote.

Her charm and quiet demeanor made Lucy Stone particularly effective on the lecture platform. She was seldom rattled by opposition or personal abuse.

One day she was drenched by a hose sprayed at her from behind while she was speaking. She quietly wrapped her shawl around her shoulders and kept right on with her lecture.

When a mob attempted to break up an antislavery meeting on Cape Cod, Lucy Stone sweetly asked one of the mob leaders to permit her to speak. He stood guard while she addressed the unruly listeners from a tree stump. When she finished, the crowd took up a collection to repair the torn coat of one of the other speakers in the melee.

Later Lucy Stone described the difficulties under which she carried on her verbal battle for equal rights:

> In Hanover Street, Boston was a boarding-house kept by a very respectable retired sea-captain and his wife, where I could get meals for twelve and a half cents, and lodging for six and a quarter cents. I slept in the same bed with two of the daughters, in the attic occupied by the servants, and separated from them only by a curtain. I had some small handbills printed; and as I could not pay for posting them, I bought a paper of tacks and put up bills myself, using a stone for a hammer. A collection was taken at the close, and I went around with the hat myself. There was no one else to do it.

It was not until she was thirty-seven that Lucy Stone consented to be married—to another antislavery activist, Henry B. Blackwell. She still maintained her independence, becoming the first woman (not an actress) to continue to use her maiden name instead of adopting her husband's. At their wedding ceremony, the officiating clergyman read aloud the couple's protest against current marital laws:

> We believe that personal independence and equal human rights can never be forfeited, except for crime; that marriage should be an equal and permanent partnership, and so recognized by law.

For forty years Lucy Stone stayed in the forefront of the fight for equal rights both for blacks and for women. She fought battles against discriminatory state laws in Rhode Island, Vermont, Michigan, Kansas, Nebraska and Colorado. She edited the *Woman's Journal* for more than twenty of those years, educating and converting other women to the cause. She also served as chairman of the American Woman Suffrage Association.

When Lucy Stone died in 1893, she called her only child, Alice Stone Blackwell, to her side just before she passed away. These were her parting words: "Make the world better."

Muhammad Ali was born Cassius Marcellus Clay, Jr., in Louisville, Kentucky, in 1942. He learned to box at twelve, and fought over a hundred amateur bouts before he won the Golden Gloves light heavyweight championship in 1959. In 1960, he represented the United States at the Olympics in Rome and won a gold medal.

Following the Olympics, Clay became a professional boxer. For four grueling years he took on fighter after fighter as he inched his way toward the top. Then in 1964, Clay won the world heavyweight championship from Sonny Liston.

Now at the peak of his career, Clay suddenly announced that he had joined the Black Muslim movement, committed to black nationalism, and that he had changed his name to Muhammad Ali. Black Muslims were widely (and mistakenly) thought to be a subversive "race hate" sect. While opposed to acquiescing to white supremacy, the Muslims' goals were primarily economic, educational and spiritual self-sufficiency, and their scruples were largely puritan. The movement was gaining adherents rapidly among middle-class blacks.

Influenced by his brother, who was already a Muslim, Clay had undergone a profound spiritual and intellectual transformation.

Ali attacked United States participation in the Vietnam War. In 1967 he refused to be drafted into military service as a religious conscientious objector. The boxing authorities stripped him of his crown and his license to fight. The Illinois Athletic Commission ruled that unless he apologized for his views on the Vietnam War, Ali could never box again. He was prosecuted by the federal government for draft evasion, and sentenced to the maximum fine and imprisonment for five years—a punishment rarely meted out to even the most willful draft evader. While he appealed his case, Ali was forced to earn his living lecturing.

Finally in 1970, the Supreme Court of the United States upheld Muhammad Ali's exemption from the draft as a religious conscientious objector and reversed his conviction and sentence. Another federal court ruled that the revocation of his boxing license had been "arbitrary and unreasonable." Ali returned to the ring, and a grueling four years later, he regained the heavyweight crown at the age of thirty-two. After an intervening loss, he won the crown again in 1978, making him the first prizefighter in history to win the heavyweight championship three times.

By jeopardizing his career for his beliefs, Ali was also fighting for the dignity of black Americans. The independence and courage he demonstrated in the face of the vindictiveness of boxing authorities and Selective Service was more impressive than any of his exploits in the ring.

* * *

A college president and his brother, a New York lawyer, get their grown families together for a Fourth of July reunion at Wellfleet, Massachusetts (on Cape Cod), each year. There are usually between twelve and sixteen people present, representing three generations. After they have gathered for an evening beach picnic, with everyone seated in a semicircle, a copy of the Declaration of Independence is passed around, and each person present reads aloud a passage from the document, including the names of all the signers.

Then they talk about the various grievances described by Thomas Jefferson and his committee, and note parallels to contemporary problems. They comment on the personal risks taken by those who affixed their names publicly to the Declaration.

Every person there is reminded to keep alive the American spirit of independence, to expose wrongs, to oppose injustices. It is a frank, open and enthusiastic discussion, and its impact on the young people is visible.

Independence begins with thinking for ourselves, with making our own decisions about what is right and what is wrong. It often requires affirmative action, making a personal declaration of independence by what we do. Like Thoreau going to jail to make a point. Like Prudence Crandall defying bigotry in the most forceful way she could. Like Lucy Stone using her own life to disprove the ignorant prejudices of her elders. Like Muhammad Ali enduring the hate and resentment of much of the nation in order to stand by his religious convictions. These are examples of independence of heroic proportions which have added nobility to the human race.

Independence is not easy. Most of us care deeply about the opinions of our peers. We are eager to please, to gain acceptance, to win approval. We bunch together like sheep, trying hard not to give offense or call attention to ourselves. We go along with the crowd.

For elected officials, survival in office generally depends on pleasing as many constituents as possible, the exact reverse of being independent. When officeholders display real independence, they are usually rewarded by a primary opponent, adverse editorials, or a strong opposition candidate in the general election.

For people climbing up the ladder in business, academia, government, public institutions, large law firms—almost everywhere—keeping your nose to the grindstone and not rocking the boat are safe formulas for getting ahead.

The antithesis is true freedom—the freedom to do what we believe is right. Independence means marching to our own drummer. Damn the torpedoes—full speed ahead.

Independence is a precious resource. It should not be squandered. Choose your timing with care. Use your judgment, so that when you express an independent opinion or head off in a different direction from the crowd, you will accomplish something worthwhile.

Take a stand for things that really matter. Let the trivial issues go by, lest you impair your effectiveness and fritter away your strongest asset.

When the right moment comes, be prepared to step out without hesitation. Do what you *know* is right. Do not look back over your shoulder. Just put your head down and go.

You will experience an exhilaration that has no equal, as you put into practice and make real your convictions and beliefs.

Independence is a rough and lonely road. Be prepared to travel the full distance.

During the Civil War, Secretary of the Army Stanton complained to Abraham Lincoln about the Commander in Chief's overruling of military experts at a time when the Union Army was suffering a series of defeats. Stanton told the President that his actions were costing him the support of many friends in the administration. Replied Lincoln:

> Mr. Secretary, even though I lose every other friend on earth, I will still have one friend left—deep down inside me.

Help Yourself First

Best place to look for helping hand—at end
of right arm.

—Chinese fortune cookie

For years Benjamin Franklin planned to write a book
on *The Art of Virtue.* It is too bad his other projects
pushed that one aside. Franklin had a unique understanding of human frailties and the need for overcoming them. Witness these gems from issues of his *Poor
Richard's Almanac:*

Do good to thy friend to keep him;
to thy enemy to gain him. (1734)

He that can have patience can have
what he will. (1736)

If you would not be forgotten
as soon as you are dead and rotten,
either write things worth reading
or do things worth the writing. (1738)

Defer not thy well doing; be not
like St. George, who is always
a-horseback and never rides on. (1738)

An empty bag cannot stand upright. (1740)

The sleeping fox catches no poultry.
Up! Up! (1743)

Franklin was no sermonizer. He spoke from personal
experience. Criticized for overindulgence, occasional
sharp practices, and "philandering," Franklin was
still able to render outstanding public service to the
American colonies and the new nation. How he
brought his imperfections under control is a valuable
lesson in self-discipline.

Franklin was twenty when he instituted his first
self-improvement program. Following a year and a
half working as a journeyman printer in London, he
returned to Philadelphia by ship and used the long
ocean journey to reflect on his personal habits. Carl
Van Doren, Franklin's biographer, says the rules the
young Philadelphian set for himself during the journey included the following:

1. Stay out of Debt.
2. Always Speak the Truth.
3. Never Speak Ill of Others.
4. Work Hard and Do Not Be Diverted by Foolish
   Projects.

Upon his arrival in Philadelphia, young Franklin
made a detailed list of the personal virtues in which he
was deficient—a total of thirteen—writing them in a
notebook, each one on a separate page. For a week

at a time he concentrated on strengthening himself in a single virtue. Franklin calculated that he could go through the entire cycle of thirteen virtues four times every year, continuing on as long as necessary. At the end of each day he jotted down in his notebook the number of times he had failed to conform to that virtue during the day. His goal was to achieve a clean sheet on every page.

The specific virtues Franklin listed in his notebook were these:

1. *Temperance:* Eat not to dullness; drink not to elevation.
2. *Silence:* Speak not but what may benefit others or yourself; avoid trifling conversation.
3. *Order:* Let all your things have their places; let each part of your business have its time.
4. *Resolution:* Resolve to perform what you ought; perform without fail what you resolve.
5. *Frugality:* Make no expense but to do good to others or yourself; i.e., waste nothing.
6. *Industry:* Lose no time; be always employed in something useful; cut off all unnecessary actions.
7. *Sincerity:* Use no hurtful deceit; think innocently and justly, and, if you speak, speak accordingly.
8. *Justice:* Wrong none by doing injuries, or omitting the benefits that are your duty.
9. *Moderation:* Avoid extremes; forbear resenting injuries so much as you think they deserve.
10. *Cleanliness:* Tolerate no uncleanliness in body, clothes, or habitation.
11. *Tranquillity:* Be not disturbed at trifles, or at accidents common or unavoidable.
12. *Chastity:* Rarely use venery but for health or off-

spring, never to dullness, weakness, or the injury of your own or another's peace or reputation.

13. *Humility:* Imitate Jesus and Socrates.

Franklin later wrote in his *Autobiography* that the last virtue, *Humility,* was added after a Quaker friend told him that his friends thought him "proud" and his conversation overbearing and insolent. Franklin recounts that he immediately adopted a practice never to contradict others and not to be aggressive when stating his own position:

> The modest way in which I proposed my opinions procured them a readier reception and less contradiction; I had less mortification when I was found to be in the wrong; and I more easily prevailed with others to give up their mistakes and join with me when I happened to be in the right.

(He confided, however, that he never did succeed in actually *becoming* humble, only in giving the appearance of humility—which still produced the desired results.)

Although each of us probably has a different list, the Franklin technique is worth trying. While it is not necessary to be saintly to live a full life, we cannot get very far without having the personal respect of our peers. Franklin's approach is one way to win it.

Franklin adhered to a rigorous daily schedule:

5 A.M.	Rise, wash, plan the day's work. Study. Breakfast.
8 A.M.–12 noon	Work at business.
12 noon–2 P.M.	Read. Lunch. Look after accounts.
2 P.M.–6 P.M.	Work at business.
6 P.M.–10 P.M.	Supper. Music, diversion, conversation. "Examination of the day."
10 P.M.–5 A.M.	Sleep.

By following his daily program of self-discipline, Franklin was able to grow prosperous, contribute significantly to science, and become a leader in civic and government reforms. He earned enough from his printing enterprises *by the age of forty-two* that he was able to give full time to learning and public service until his death at eighty-four, becoming the Grand Old Man of American Independence, and conducting the new nation's foreign relations at a level of personal diplomacy that has never been equaled. His many contributions to science and public affairs were directly rooted in his personal program of self-discipline.

Franklin's contemporary and admirer Thomas Jefferson was asked in 1825, shortly before his death, to write a letter of personal advice to an infant namesake, Thomas Jefferson Smith. Jefferson's counsel was terse:

> Adore God.
> Reverence and cherish your parents.
> Love your neighbor as yourself, and your
>   country more than yourself.
> Be just.
> Be true.
> Murmur not at the way of Providence.

Enclosed with Jefferson's letter was a list of ten precepts ("A Decalogue of Canons") which could have been written by Franklin himself:

1. Never put off till to-morrow what you can do today.
2. Never trouble another for what you can do yourself.
3. Never spend your money before you have it.

4. Never buy what you do not want, because it is cheap; it will be dear to you.
5. Pride costs no more than hunger, thirst and cold.
6. We never repent of having eaten too little.
7. Nothing is troublesome that we do willingly.
8. How much pain have cost us the evils which have never happened.
9. Take things always by their smooth handle.
10. When angry, count ten, before you speak; if very angry, an hundred.

In 1850, Abraham Lincoln wrote notes of advice for law students which apply equally to anyone interested in developing a sound code of personal conduct:

> The leading rule for the lawyer, as for the man in every other calling, is diligence. Leaving nothing for tomorrow which can be done today. Never let your correspondence fall behind. Whatever piece of business you have in hand, before stopping, do all the labor pertaining to it which can then be done.... There is a vague popular belief that lawyers are necessarily dishonest.... Let no young man choosing the law for a calling for a moment yield to the popular belief—resolve to be honest at all events; and if in your own judgment you cannot be an honest lawyer, resolve to be honest without being a lawyer. Choose some other occupation, rather than one in the choosing of which you do, in advance, consent to be a knave.

Winston Churchill was acutely aware of a chronic habit of tardiness, no matter how important the occasion. In his autobiography, *A Roving Commission: My Early Life*, Churchill recounted an experience he had as a young second lieutenant in the British Army when invited to a dinner party for the Prince of Wales. The dinner was at a great house in the country, and it was necessary for young Winston to travel there by train. The guests included his commanding officer, so Churchill knew he would have to be on his best behavior ("punctual, subdued, reserved—all the qualities with which I am least endowed"). He caught the 7:15 P.M. train, then realized that even if the train was exactly on time he would be late for dinner, scheduled for eight-thirty. The train was not on time; it ran increasingly behind schedule as it plodded from station to station:

> When I arrived at Deepdene, I found the entire company assembled in the drawing room. The party it seemed without me would be only thirteen. The prejudice of the Royal Family of those days against sitting down thirteen is well known. The Prince had refused point-blank to go in, and would not allow any re-arrangement of the tables to be made. He had, as was his custom, been punctual to the minute at half-past eight. It was now twelve minutes to nine. There, in this large room, stood this select and distinguished company in the worst of tempers, and there on the other hand was I, a young boy asked as a special favour and compliment.... "Don't they teach you to be punctual in your regiment, Winston?" said the Prince in his most severe tone, and then looked acidly at Colonel Brabazon, who glowered. It was an awful moment!

The experience did not break Churchill's habit:

> I do think unpunctuality is a vile habit and all my life I have tried to break myself of it. "I have never been able," said Dr. Welldon to me some years later, "to understand the point of view of persons who make a practice of being ten minutes late for each of a series

of appointments throughout the day." I entirely agree
with this dictum. The only straight-forward course is
to cut out one or two of the appointments altogether
and so catch up. But very few men have the strength of
mind to do this.

Tardy or not, Sir Winston was the one man who rallied
the free world through his remarkable personal leadership at a crucial moment when Nazi Germany was
poised to invade and overrun England during World
War II. That service may well have preserved democ-
racy in modern times. It mattered not that he had bad
personal habits. What mattered was that he had the
character and spirit to stand up when he was needed.

Franklin Delano Roosevelt brought vision and com-
passion to public policy during the Great Depression,
and changed the role of the national government from
that of bystander to active participant in the welfare
of the country. Although many disagreed with FDR's
policies, the impact of his administration on the nation
and the world cannot be underestimated.

Five years after the death of the former President,
John Gunther summed up his personality in the opening chapter of *Roosevelt in Retrospect*. After listing
FDR's strong points, Gunther set forth a list of his
negative characteristics:

> He had plenty of bad qualities—dilatoriness, two-
> sidedness (some critics would say plain dishonesty),
> pettiness in some personal relationships, a cardinal
> lack of frankness (for which, however, there was often
> good reason), inability to say No, love of improvisa-
> tion, garrulousness, amateurism, and what has been
> called "cheerful vindictiveness."

These qualities did not interfere with Roosevelt's commitment to public service, or diminish his many farsighted contributions to the welfare of his fellow Americans.

The examples of Churchill and FDR are good reminders that we are all human creatures with human faults. Striving to control those faults is a continuing challenge, but these faults should not prevent us from tackling major responsibilities when opportunity comes.

General of the Army Douglas MacArthur, World War II Commander of United States Forces in the Pacific Theater of Operations, was an "army brat," brought up on military posts. Much of his formal education was received at his mother's knee. She drummed into him a set of ethical standards:

> Our teaching included not only the simple rudiments, but above all else, a sense of obligation. We were to do what was right no matter what the personal sacrifice might be. Our country was always to come first. Two things we must never do: never lie, never tattle.

When MacArthur prepared for his competitive exams for appointment to West Point, he recalled his mother's instructions:

> The night before the examination, for the first time in my life I could not sleep, and the next morning when I arrived at the city hall I felt nauseated. But the cool words of my mother brought me around. "Doug," she said, "you'll win if you don't lose your nerve. You must believe in yourself, my son, or no one else will be-

lieve in you. Be self-confident, self-reliant, and even if
you don't make it, you will know that you have done
your best. Now, go to it." When the marks were
counted, I led. My careful preparation had repaid me.
It was a lesson I never forgot. Preparedness is the key
to success and victory.

From his father MacArthur learned that there are
limits to the effectiveness of self-discipline, no matter
how good your intentions may be.

Toward the end of the Civil War, his father told
him, the Union general in charge of the occupied terri-
tory surrounding New Orleans was pressed by local
plantation owners to permit them to haul their cotton
to the wharves so they could be sold for shipment to
England. The general controlled all the wagons and
horses, and his explicit orders from high command in
Washington were not to let the cotton crop get to market. He enforced them to the letter.

Then one day, when Colonel Arthur MacArthur
was visiting the general, two Southern ladies were
ushered into the general's office, one a *grande dame*,
the other a young beauty. The older lady came right to
the point: The landowners needed the temporary use of
transport facilities to move their cotton. The North did
not wish to force England into the war, she said, and
was allowing blockade running and therefore would
not be opposed to the sale of cotton for English textile mills. To show their gratitude she handed over
$250,000 in gold certificates. "And if you need other
inducements, this young lady will supply them."
Thereupon they departed, leaving behind the young
lady's address.

The general immediately dictated the following
dispatch to MacArthur:

TO THE PRESIDENT OF THE UNITED STATES:
I have just been offered two hundred and fifty thousand dollars and the most beautiful woman I have ever seen to betray my trust. I am depositing the money with the Treasury of the United States, and request immediate relief from this command. They are getting close to my price.

Virtue has no price. Its practice depends entirely on personal determination.

When Franklin Delano Roosevelt arrived at the White House in 1933, America was well into the Great Depression. In those dark days, the new President told the American people a story about one of his predecessors, Andrew Jackson, known affectionately to his friends as "Old Hickory" because of his legendary strong will. FDR said that "Jackson never would give up." One of Jackson's schoolmates bragged that he was able to "throw him three times out of four" in a fight, but complained that "he would never *stay* throwed."

At the time of Jackson's death, according to Roosevelt, someone inquired of one of his friends: "Will Andrew Jackson go to heaven?"

Came the unhesitating response: "He will if he *wants* to." FDR continued:

> If I am asked whether the American people will pull themselves out of this Depression, I answer, "They will if they want to."

"Wanting to" is a principal ingredient in fashioning a full life. Every one of us has to grapple with personality flaws which we too often perceive as deep character defects. Franklin did. Jefferson did. Lincoln did. Churchill. MacArthur. Roosevelt.

The trick is not to let these deficiencies become *excuses* for inaction. Too often we blame "Providence" for making us indolent or selfish or dawdling, and we view these normal tendencies as permanent conditions which make it impossible for us to achieve the goals which "better" people do achieve.

But there are no "better" people. There are only those who *try harder* to bring their share of human traits under reasonable control. They try harder because they *want* to. It is a state of mind.

Oliver Wendell Holmes, Senior, the self-described "autocrat" of the breakfast table, told his son he only needed "fire in the belly" to succeed. Succeed he did. Other fathers have given that same good advice to their offspring. Heed it now.

One useful device is to look for *corners* to turn in our own lives, corners which give an opportunity to begin afresh. The corners can be simple—like a vacation, New Year's Day, a birthday. Or they can be major—a new job, a new home, a new community.

Turning each corner provides a chance to change your patterns of behavior: to get up earlier in the morning; to walk a mile every day on the way to work; to make a "to do" list every night before going to bed.

That is the way Benjamin Franklin did it. He turned a corner as he went from London back to Philadelphia, and made his own punch list of new habits he wanted to cultivate—"virtues" that would make him more effective, more efficient, more agreeable, more respected. He obviously did not achieve them all, but he tried, and he made remarkable progress.

We can each do the same.

Act Quickly and Decisively

By and by never comes.

—St. Augustine

A day's impact is better than a month of dead pull.

—Justice Oliver Wendell Holmes, Jr.

D.I.N.

—A family motto*

When Harriet Beecher Stowe was visiting her clergyman brother in Boston in 1840, she listened to Josiah Henson, a former slave, describe how, when he was a child, he had watched his father die from a beating by a cruel plantation overseer. The description of the incident moved Mrs. Stowe deeply, and she thought about it often after her return to Maine.

One Sunday morning while she was in church, her mind began to wander during the sermon, and she vi-

---

* Do it now.

sualized the slave-beating episode. The moment the
service was over, Mrs. Stowe went home, shut herself in
her room, and started writing out the violent scene as
she pictured it. She soon ran out of paper. After
searching the house, she opened up wrapping paper in
which she had brought home her groceries and used it
to complete her writing.

Harriet Beecher Stowe wrote the central scene of
Uncle Tom's Cabin in half a day. The book would soon
become the most powerful antislavery document in
America's history.

Melvil Dewey went to Amherst College. While he was
an undergraduate he became agitated by the lack of
consistency and organization in the research libraries
he used. Each library had its own system of cataloging
and classification. No two were alike. The duplication
of effort and inefficiency hounded him.

As for Harriet Stowe, a dull sermon provided the
needed catalyst. One Sunday morning, Dewey's mind
turned to the library enigma during a particularly
long sermon. In a flash, it occurred to him that libraries could develop uniformity by using Arabic nu-
merals instead of words for their classification system.
Using the Amherst library as his guinea pig, he set to
work developing and perfecting his idea.

Two years later, aged twenty-four, Melvil Dewey
published the first edition of his subject index classification system, *Decimal Classifications and Relative
Index,* which has become the standard for libraries
throughout the English-speaking world.

Dewey soon turned to organizing libraries into the
American Library Association, serving as its first secretary. Then he became librarian of Columbia College,

in 1883, where he established the first library school in the country, overcoming opposition from the college's administrators to the admission of women.

When Dewey later was selected to be director of the New York State Library in Albany, he drafted the legislation to establish a state library system which is still the governing law for New York's public libraries.

Dewey met his match when he attempted to reform the English language. He developed a method to simplify the spelling of words which were unnecessarily complex. He calculated that three years could be saved in a child's education by using his simplified spelling plan. Meanwhile, he and his wife founded the Lake Placid Club where he tested out his spelling theories on the menus. One visitor commented that after a short stay at the Lake Placid Club, "A guest would have trouble spelling 'mayonnaise' for the rest of his or her life."

One Sunday during the early days of the Civil War, a forty-four-year-old widow, Mary Bickerdyke, was attending church services in Galesburg, Illinois. The pastor, the Reverend Edward Beeche, told the congregation about the wretched living conditions for recruits at a military camp downstate near Cairo which was rife with typhoid and dysentery. He urged his parishioners to organize a relief fund. Mary Bickerdyke stepped forward. She volunteered to oversee the distribution of the fund's proceeds at the camp and started to take up a collection.

When Mrs. Bickerdyke arrived at the Cairo encampment on June 9, 1861, she found tents crowded with patients, living under intolerable sanitary and dietary conditions. She set to work feeding and caring for the sick men. Soon she was asked to take complete charge of the camp hospital. Her stay in Cairo extended to nine months.

As the fighting spread into the Midwest, Mary Bickerdyke made trips to the battlefields to help evacuate the wounded. After the battle of Shiloh in April 1862, she spent seven months working in Union field hospitals caring for the wounded and dying. She arranged food preparation, distribution of supplies, laundry and other sanitary services, all the while making the best of rudimentary equipment.

"Mother" Bickerdyke (as the soldiers called her) was given increasing responsibility, and by early 1863 was asked to take charge of sanitary conditions at the large military hospital in Memphis, Tennessee. Upon her arrival she discovered that the hospital diet was meager and unappetizing and decided to take direct action. She made her way to Illinois and asked farmers for contributions of cows and chickens, which she transported back to the hospital grounds to ensure a steady supply of fresh milk and eggs for her patients.

When one regular army doctor mistakenly challenged her right to make a particular decision and demanded to know the source of her authority, Mrs. Bickerdyke's response thundered through camp:

"On the authority of Lord God Almighty. Have you anything that outranks that?"

Cornelia Hancock tried to enlist as an army nurse in Philadelphia after she read about the bloodbath at Gettysburg. She was rejected on the ground that she was too young, but proceeded to Gettysburg anyway, on her own, arriving on the third day after the battle.

She started carrying food to the hundreds of wounded soldiers still lying on the ground. By the end of three weeks she was in charge of eight tents of amputees.

As each of these examples shows, the key to getting results is getting under way. If you have a desire to do something, you must also find the drive to get it done. That drive usually comes when inspiration is strongest—at the very start. Delay invariably saps energy and enthusiasm. Beware those who counsel postponement, for they usually are counseling inaction. The ancient fable of the tortoise and the hare still has lessons for us all.

Winifred Holt was attending a concert in Italy with her sister, Edith, one evening in 1901, when they both observed a group of young blind students who were deeply absorbed in the performance and enjoying it immensely. Daughters of a successful New York publisher, the well-bred girls had gone to Italy to study sculpture, drawing and music. After the concert, the two sisters discussed what they had seen, and decided they should find a way to help blind people in America enjoy music and theater.

After their return home to New York, Winifred and Edith Holt organized a meeting in their family's home to establish the New York Association for the Blind, with Winifred Holt agreeing to serve as secretary and principal fund raiser. In 1913, the association opened an educational, employment and recreational center for the blind, called The Lighthouse. An exhibition and sale of blind workers' products was held at the Metropolitan Opera House. The center was an instant success and continues so to this day.

In time, Winifred Holt helped to establish the first Lighthouses in France, England, Poland, Italy, India and China. (She also pressed for public-school education for blind children alongside sighted children, and made the time to establish the first Braille magazine for children.)

In 1907, Emily Perkins Bissell was asked by a physician cousin to help raise funds for a much-needed care facility for tuberculosis patients in Wilmington, Delaware. She had just read a magazine article by Jacob Riis in *The Outlook* in which he described the sale of "Christmas stamps" by the Danish government each year to raise funds to fight TB, and decided to copy the idea to fund the Delaware treatment facility.

Ms. Bissell enlisted the cooperation of the local Red Cross (which gave permission to use its logo), the advertising office of E. I. du Pont, de Nemours and Company (which provided the artwork), a local printer (who produced the stamps on a rush basis), and the Wilmington postmaster (who permitted the sale of the stamps in the post office lobby). When it became obvious that the rate of sales at one cent per stamp would not bring in sufficient revenue to meet her goal, Emily Bissell went to Philadelphia and set up a second sales table in the main post office there. Since that first year's success, funds received from sales of TB Christmas Seals have helped virtually to eradicate tuberculosis in America.

During World War I, a cafeteria operator in Muskogee, Oklahoma, decided it would be a nice idea to sup-

ply hot coffee to soldiers on the troop trains that
stopped at the railroad depot on their way through
town. Alice Mary Robertson was soon driving her
Model T Ford to the station at virtually every hour of
the day and night to meet troop trains. She became a
legend among the soldiers. Citizens in other railroad
towns began to copy her. Eventually the idea led to the
founding of a national program to help servicemen
away from home—the USO.

In May 1929, Abby Aldrich Rockefeller invited Lizzie
Plummer Bliss and Mary Quinn Sullivan to join her
for lunch. All three women were interested in Impres-
sionist, Cubist and Abstract art, and had each assembled important private collections. Over lunch they
discussed the need to encourage public support for
modern art, and agreed that New York City should
have a museum dedicated solely to it. They decided to
enlist an organizing committee. A. Conger Goodyear
agreed to become chairman. A charter was drawn up
and signed by seven trustees. By November they had
hired a director, Alfred Barr, and had organized an exhibition in rented quarters of works by Cézanne, Gau-
guin, Seurat and Van Gogh.

When Mrs. Bliss died of cancer, she left her entire
collection of 150 works of modern art to the fledgling
organization on condition that a museum be established on a "firm financial basis" within three years.
Responding to the challenge, the trustees set to work
and raised $600,000. So began one of the world's most
important art museums, New York's Museum of Modern Art. Even in cultural affairs, acting quickly and
decisively is what makes the difference.

* * *

One of the giants in United States constitutional history was "The Great Dissenter," Oliver Wendell Holmes, Jr., Associate Justice of the Supreme Court of the United States. During most of the first half of the twentieth century, Holmes was frequently the sole voice of reason against the ultraconservative and reactionary members of America's highest court. While his colleagues repeatedly blocked attempts to improve working conditions, restrain business excesses, and protect the right of free speech, Holmes singlehandedly defended the Constitution as a living document whose provisions needed to adapt to meet changing conditions in each new generation. In a stinging dissent in *Abrams* v. *United States,* when the Court's majority upheld twenty-year prison sentences for five self-described "anarchists" who had distributed handbills entitled "The Hypocrisy of the United States and Her Allies," criticizing the sending of United States troops into Russia, Holmes spoke of the Constitution as follows: "It is an experiment, as all life is an experiment."

Justice Holmes called for "free trade in ideas," and in just twenty-one words stated the entire premise that lies behind the Constitution's guarantee of freedom of speech and press:

> The best test of truth is the power of the thought to get itself accepted in the competition of the market. . . .

(As with many other Holmes dissents, his minority view has since become the majority view of the Supreme Court on the meaning of the Constitution.)

While other justices would take weeks or months to write their opinions, Holmes's practice was to get to work immediately after the weekly conference of the Court, at which opinion-writing assignments were made by the Chief Justice. Holmes wrote his opinions himself in longhand, using a stand-up desk (which helped keep his opinions short). He read all of the briefs submitted by the lawyers, as well as all of the leading cases cited as precedent. He made time for these tasks by rarely reading newspapers or magazines. Holmes usually completed all his opinion-writing assignments between Saturday morning and Monday noon, leaving a clean desk ready to tackle another group of cases as soon as the new week began.

Holmes was a young man during the Civil War and served in the Union Army. The tale is that one day Abraham Lincoln visited the front and Holmes was assigned as his aide-de-camp to accompany him on an inspection of the Union lines. At one point the President climbed up on the ramparts to look across at the enemy lines not many yards away, and made a perfect target. There was a rattle of musket fire. Holmes quickly seized his Commander-in-Chief by his arm and pulled him to safety, shouting, "Get down, you fool!"

As soon as he realized what he had said, Holmes started worrying about his impertinence, and fully expected to be reprimanded.

As Lincoln prepared to depart at the end of his visit, he turned to the young officer with a smile and said, "I'm glad to see you know how to talk to a civilian."

One day during the late 1940s, Richard Rodgers and Oscar Hammerstein II asked Irving Berlin to join

them for lunch at the Algonquin Hotel in New York.
The two producers told Berlin how they had hired an
old friend, Jerome Kern, to write the music and lyrics
for a new musical show they were working on, based
on the life of the famous woman sharpshooter Annie
Oakley. Kern had died unexpectedly. Would he help
them out?

Berlin was dubious. "Hillbilly music" was not his
style. He would think about it.

The meeting took place on Friday. The three men
agreed to meet again the following Monday. Berlin, his
wife, and their three daughters headed off to spend the
weekend at their farm in the Catskills. As soon as they
arrived there, Berlin started studying the outline for
the show. Monday noon, when he met with Rodgers and
Hammerstein, he tried out a couple of numbers he had
composed over the weekend. One was "You Can't Get a
Man with a Gun"; the other, "They Say It's Wonderful." Both were destined to become top hits in the
long-run Broadway musical *Annie Get Your Gun.*
They were the result of one weekend's efforts.

One family whose members are constantly involved in
good works—historic preservation, environmental conservation, *pro bono* legal work, constitutional battles,
housing, the arts—has a curious habit of quoting mot-
toes to each other:

He who hesitates is lost.

When opportunity knocks, open the door and offer her
a chair.

Do it now.

The last—"Do it now"—is the family's creed.
  They say it repeatedly.
  They follow it.
  It works.

What are you planning to accomplish next weekend?

Cultivating an Affirmative Attitude

C H A P T E R   4

Commitment

Never give up! Never, never, never give up!

—WINSTON CHURCHILL

Few things are harder to put up with than the annoyance of a good example.

—MARK TWAIN

George Washington Carver was born a slave toward the end of the Civil War. His father was killed in an accident and the boy was raised by his owner's family, whose name he adopted. Bright and responsive, he soon outgrew the educational opportunities of rural Missouri. At the age of fourteen, he went to Kansas, where he received high-school training. After a brief period of homesteading, he made his way to Iowa. There he earned a degree from a small college while working in a laundry.

George Carver then enrolled in the Iowa State College of Agriculture at Ames, where he studied the science of plant fertilization and propagation. He received a master's degree in bacterial botany from Ames in 1896.

He planned to continue his graduate study, but

was sidetracked by a letter from Booker T. Washington at Tuskegee Institute in southern Alabama. The letter invited Carver to join Tuskegee's staff to give the school a capability in agricultural science. In the letter Washington said:

> I offer you ... work—hard, hard work—the task of bringing a people from degradation, poverty and waste to full manhood.

George Washington Carver could not resist the entreaty. He arrived on the Tuskegee campus a few months later to begin an association which was to last forty-seven years—right up until his death. Carver's salary was fixed at $125 per month, and it never changed over the entire period. His responsibilities included teaching and playing the piano for concerts to help raise funds for the institution.

Shortly after his arrival, in the spring of 1897, Carver asked permission to develop twenty acres of gullied, sandy soil as an experimental farm. Using makeshift equipment, Carver raised the soil's productivity by planting cowpeas to add nitrogen to the soil. This and other successful experiments led him to conclude that the poverty of most black farmers resulted from lack of crop diversification, poor soil conservation, and inadequate promotion and utilization of farm products.

Carver began to urge neighboring farmers to plant peanuts, sweet potatoes, cowpeas and other neglected crops in the place of cotton. He experimented with ways to eliminate diseases from the crops, and searched for new end uses for them.

Carver inaugurated a traveling agricultural

school to demonstrate agricultural methods to black farmers throughout the Southeast. He conducted seminars and conferences at Tuskegee aimed at improving both agriculture and nutrition.

His experiments with alternative uses for the peanut produced over 300 different possibilities, including peanut oil, various food products and plastics. Carver identified 118 different products which could be produced from the sweet potato, 75 from the pecan.

Despite the originality of his work, Carver never patented his ideas, believing that they should be made available as widely as possible.

Working entirely alone, with only occasional student assistance, far outside the mainstream of contemporary scientific research, George Washington Carver made a series of important discoveries which brought him honors from many quarters in the United States and Great Britain.

Other research laboratories tried to hire him away. Thomas Edison tried. So did several industrialists. But Carver was committed to his own cause— helping his people make better use of their resources, and expanding the market for their products.

When he died George Washington Carver's will directed that his small estate be used to provide advanced study for black youths in botany, chemistry and agronomy.

The year 1905 marked the beginning of the "Einstein Revolution," with the appearance in a German journal of the brilliant young scientist's first writing on the theory of relativity. It challenged all the accepted concepts of matter and energy, time and space. Albert

Einstein asserted that all motion is relative, while the speed of light is always constant. The movement of light, he said, was the only unvarying factor in the entire universe.

Following this first publication, Einstein continued to enlarge on his theory. In his second article he presented the "Einstein equation," which supplied the key to atomic energy:

$$E = mc^2$$

(Energy equals mass multiplied by the speed of light, squared.) His brilliant analysis of the volume of energy that is locked up in a mass provided the foundation for all subsequent atomic research. For the first time, it quantified the amount of energy that would be released from any given mass if it could be unlocked, as in uranium.

A 1939 communication from Albert Einstein to President Franklin D. Roosevelt pointing out the significance of Enrico Fermi's experiments with an atomic pile at the University of Chicago led directly to the start of the United States research project at Los Alamos, New Mexico, that produced the world's first atom bomb.

Other Einstein research led to many extraordinary technological advances, including motion-picture sound tracks and television.

These achievements of Albert Einstein came as direct results of his commitment to a belief, despite extreme discouragement.

Einstein had been a young patent officer in Bern, Switzerland, when he first developed his theory of relativity. This development took place in 1904, shortly after his wife had given birth to their first son. He had been studying physics, and his mind was tormented by the unanswered questions that he kept finding wherever he turned. Einstein picked away at the basic concepts, believing they would lead him to greater truths.

For days on end he would concentrate on unanswered questions. Each time he solved one puzzle, he found another. He stopped eating. He stopped sleeping. He kept pushing his quest into the nature of matter and the speed of light.

Meanwhile, as the young scientist was grappling with underlying theoretical questions, he was making incidental discoveries of major importance: molecular dimensions (which later won him his Ph.D. degree), and the quantum theory of light (a beam of light is in reality a shower of particles, rather than waves of light, as other scientists maintained).

Einstein was not satisfied with these results. He believed there was something more. He wrestled with his questions constantly, working himself into a state of exhaustion. He wandered through the countryside, took days off from the office, worked at many mathematical calculations—but still he could not find the answer he was sure was eluding him.

One night Einstein decided he should give up. He told himself he would never be able to unravel the mystery, and so he concluded it was time to stop. The prospect of relief from his labors brought sudden relaxation to his exhausted brain. He went to bed. As he slept, the missing portions of the theory suddenly fell into place. When he awoke, he realized that he had at last discovered nature's most carefully guarded secret.

The twenty-six-year-old civil servant immediately set to work putting his theory down on paper. For five weeks he worked almost around the clock, producing thirty pages of text he would entitle "On the Electrodynamics of Bodies in Motion." There was not a single footnote or reference source. All of it was original work.

When he finished the last entry in his paper, Einstein literally collapsed from fatigue. He spent two weeks in bed recuperating. Through sheer personal commitment he had produced a new insight into the nature of matter which would change the entire direction of the world's scientific thinking.

Writers, artists, composers and poets in particular need commitment if they hope to make significant contributions in their fields. Stories of how creative people have overcome obstacles to produce their work are marvelous displays of endurance and commitment. Yet the circumstances in which such artists work are usually little different from those under which all of us exist. It is the unswerving commitment of such people which makes it possible for them to make the time, find the inspiration, and seize the moment to put pencil to paper and turn out creative work.

Author Louis Auchincloss is a practicing lawyer in New York City. He makes time to write his novels by thinking through plots and passages while riding the subway to and from his office. On Saturday mornings he sits down with a yellow pad and pencil, and writes out the material he has worked up during the week.

Thornton Wilder used a variant of this approach by taking long solitary walks, away from all distractions and interruptions, and composing pages of dialogue in his head.

Wallace Stevens was a lawyer employed by the Hartford Accident and Indemnity Company to handle insurance claims. Despite his full-time job, he found time to write exquisite verse for which he won two National Book Awards and a Pulitzer Prize. He composed many of his poems in his head while walking from his house to "The Rock," the company's granite home-office building.

Opera composer Richard Owen is a United States district judge in New York. He writes prizewinning modern operatic works, such as *A Fisherman Called Peter*, *Mary Dyer* and *The Death of the Virgin*, on weekends and during summer vacations. What is extraordinary about Judge Owen is that he had no formal music training until after he had graduated from law school. He taught himself to play the piano by setting his alarm clock for 5:30 A.M. every day so that he could get in two hours of practice before heading off to his job downtown. He composed his first one-act opera while he was serving as an assistant United States attorney. Most of the judge's professional career has been spent in public service at a bare-bones level of compensation; he has rendered a second public service in music at the price of great personal inconvenience, with no hope of reward beyond personal satisfaction. That is true commitment.

One of the most original American poets of the twentieth century was Dr. William Carlos Williams, a pediatrician who practiced in Rutherford, New Jersey.

Dr. Williams composed his poetry in his study late at night or early in the morning, when his wife and children were sleeping. He grabbed moments in the office between patients. Sometimes he pulled his Ford over to the side of the road to scribble words on prescription blanks between house calls. The doctor-poet decided on his life-style while he was still in medical school at the University of Pennsylvania. He wanted to write but had no money:

> I was determined to be a poet; only medicine, a job I enjoyed, would make it possible for me to live and write as I wanted to. I would live: that first, and write, by God, as I wanted to, if it took me all eternity to accomplish my design.

Rufus Jones wrote and published one book every year for more than fifty years. A Quaker leader, Jones's job required him to attend countless meetings, make frequent speeches, organize conferences, and edit *American Friend.* When an interviewer later asked him how he had found time to write so many books, Jones replied: "I wrote my books on Tuesdays."

Throughout his career, Jones had simply set aside each Tuesday as his free day. When that day arrived, he sat down in his study after breakfast and wrote until dark. He used free moments during the rest of the week to think about his current writing project. When the following Tuesday morning came, he was primed and ready to go.

In the field of contemporary creative art, composer Charles Edward Ives is a perfect example of commitment. All Ives's musical work was composed with no expectation that it would ever be performed in public. It was written simply to satisfy an inner drive.

Charles Ives was born in Danbury, Connecticut, and studied music under his father, a bandmaster and music teacher. His father often played two different melodies simultaneously, each in a different key. "Stretch your ears," he told his son.

Young Ives grew accustomed to musical dissonances. For years he carried with him a childhood memory of hearing two marching bands in a parade playing different tunes at the same time. The combination of sounds had given him a very special pleasure.

Ives became a talented organist and pianist, but had no interest in playing conventional music for a livelihood. When he graduated from Yale College in 1898, he went to work for an insurance firm and soon organized his own insurance agency. He made his living selling insurance for his entire productive career. Meanwhile, at the end of each day he would sit down at his piano and write powerful music built on discords and counterthemes. Mrs. Ives protected her husband from the usual household distractions so he could work without interruption, often continuing into the small hours of the morning. At times their small daughter was permitted to sit underneath the piano and play with her dolls while her father composed, provided she did not make a sound.

Charles Ives lived this double life as insurance executive and composer of music for twenty years, from 1900 to 1920, filling reams of musical scores with his unusual compositions. Soon there were bales of scores piled up in the upstairs rooms, in the barn, in his office.

In 1918, Ives suffered a serious heart attack, later complicated by diabetes, and these illnesses forced him to give up his composing.

Twenty years after he had ceased composing, Ives began to receive professional recognition. The first complete public performance of his formidable piano composition, Sonata No. 2, "Concord, Mass.," took place on January 20, 1939. A leading music critic described it as:

> Exceptionally great music—it is, indeed, the greatest music composed by an American, and the most deeply and essentially American in impulse and implication.

Charles Ives later received the Pulitzer Prize for his Symphony No. 3 (and characteristically sent the prize money to a struggling younger composer).

One of the talented young composers Charles Ives befriended during this period was sixteen-year-old Elliott Carter, a student at the Horace Mann School in New York. Carter's music teacher, Clifton Furness, was a friend of Ives's, and Ives invited Furness and his student to join him in his box at a Saturday afternoon concert in Carnegie Hall. Serge Koussevitzky, a champion of advanced music, was conducting the Boston Symphony. Carter, a talented piano student with no particular interest in the classical works he had been studying, was overwhelmed:

> Going to these concerts with Ives and Furness, I became immediately interested in modern music. Up to that time, I had been quite bored with any kind of music, never having heard any modern music. I remember later taking my father to hear a performance

of *The Rite of Spring* and his saying that "only a madman" could have written anything like that.

Elliott Carter tried his hand at writing a complicated piano sonata and some other pieces, which he showed to Charles Ives. Ives was impressed and urged Carter to become a composer, notwithstanding expected opposition from the boy's parents.

In 1960, Elliott Carter won the Pulitzer Prize for music for his Quartet No. 2. In 1973, he won another Pulitzer Prize for his Quartet No. 3.

During the period before he himself was discovered, Charles Ives had privately printed two of his own compositions and given them away to friends. He also had published a volume of essays, which bore the following dedication:

> These prefatory essays were written by the composer for those who can't stand his music, and the music for those who can't stand his essays; to those who can't stand either, the whole is respectfully dedicated.

New Year's Day is the traditional time for making resolutions to do better. How often those resolutions are abandoned in too short a time—because they lack commitment.

The hardest part about resolving to do public service is sticking with it, especially when the going gets tough and other demands begin competing for attention.

The only remedy is commitment. We must feel so strongly about what we are trying to accomplish, so determined to getting it done, that we simply will not give up, not out of despair, not out of boredom, not out of frustration, not out of loss of heart.

"Court reform is no sport for the short-winded," Arthur Vanderbilt, chief justice of New Jersey, once observed. The same is true for any form of public service that carries no rewards beyond the satisfaction of doing what we believe is right.

Commitment comes from within. No one can give it to us, we have to make the decision ourselves.

During the 1960s, early in the environmental movement in the United States, a state legislator in New York proposed a series of laws to curb litter, especially bottles and cans mindlessly dumped along highways. To dramatize the extent of the problem he took his family out one weekend to a stretch of Route 9W near Nyack, New York, and, with the help of his wife and two children, proceeded to catalog every single piece of litter on both sides of the highway for a stretch of one tenth of a mile. They counted up cigarette butts, newspapers, beer bottles, hubcaps, tin cans—everything—then calculated the amount of litter this represented for the entire highway system of the state. An example of commitment.

The legislative proposals were ahead of their time, but the process of change had begun. Fifteen years later similar measures were enacted into law.

Perseverance

There are thousands to tell you it cannot be done,
    There are thousands to prophesy failure;
There are thousands to point out to you, one by one,
    The dangers that wait to assail you.
But just buckle in with a bit of a grin,
    Just take off your coat and go to it;
Just start to sing as you tackle the thing
    That "cannot be done," and you'll do it.

—EDGAR A. GUEST
from *Best Loved Poems*
of the American People

"Mother" Jones had a favorite expression: "The militant, not the meek, shall inherit the earth."

The petite grandmotherly figure in black dress and bonnet possibly did more to lead the way toward improved pay, hours and conditions for American workers than any other human being. Her secret weapon was perseverance. Instead of being discouraged by opposition, she thrived on it. Every roadblock to her was an opportunity, every obstacle a challenge.

It could have been otherwise, if she had not been put to the test early in her adult life.

Mary Harris Jones was simply a dutiful house-wife in 1867 when a multiple tragedy wiped out her entire family. A yellow fever epidemic sweeping through the working section of Memphis, Tennessee, took with it Mrs. Jones's four infant children and also her husband. (Mr. Jones was an organizer for an iron workers' union—one of the first successful interstate unions in the country.) The widow was broken and penniless. She returned to Chicago where she went into business as a dressmaker.

Mary Harris Jones ran her dressmaking shop for four years—until a second tragedy struck. This time it came in the form of the Chicago fire, which wiped out her shop, her work and all her belongings.

She found temporary shelter with a group of other refugees in a church. She began attending meetings of the Knights of Labor nearby (still held in secret to protect its members from employer reprisals). At the meetings she heard glowing descriptions of successful workers' organizations in Europe, heard arguments in favor of socialism, and took an increasingly active part in questioning speakers and in debates.

Before long Mary Jones started on what was to become her life's work. She was asked one day to go out to talk to groups of workers and persuade them to join the Knights of Labor. From the start she had a natural flair for the task. She projected energy and enthusi-asm. She showed a special ability to move crowds of people to action. Her particular skill was stirring people out of their apathy.

Mrs. Jones referred to herself with pride as an

"agitator" in the tradition, she said, of Jesus Christ, who "agitated against the power of Rome" and "organized the poor and the despised and the lowly." He was, she said, the "greatest agitator of all time."

She began traveling to other industrialized centers of the country, helping to unionize workers and to gather support for them when they struck for better working conditions. On one such occasion she cared for a striker whose skull had been crushed in a fight with a strikebreaker. He died in her arms. In his delirium he bagan to call Mrs. Jones "Mother." Others adopted the appellation. It stuck.

Mother Jones's most dramatic work as agitator occurred after she witnessed the working conditions for children in textile mills at Kensington, Pennsylvania. She was sickened by what she saw:

> Every day little children came into Union Headquarters, some with their hands off, some with the thumb missing, some with their fingers off at the knuckle. They were stooped little things, round shouldered and skinny.

The children usually worked ten-hour days, facing constant risk of injury from the open, unprotected machinery, and receiving substandard wages for their work tending machines, tying broken threads, and carrying large bundles of yarn.

When Mother Jones asked the local journalists why they did not publicize these appalling conditions, they responded that the millowners owned stock in their newspapers. Her reply was true to character: "Well, I've got stock in these children. I'll arrange a little publicity."

Mother Jones led the maimed factory children on a march to Oyster Bay, Long Island, summer home of President Theodore Roosevelt. The march became a national news event. *The New York Times* carried accounts every day. Meetings, rallies and press conferences were held along the route. Soon everyone knew about the child-labor conditions in Pennsylvania.

The march did its work well. The state legislature in Harrisburg quickly passed legislation prohibiting children under fourteen from performing factory work.

Mother Jones now turned her attention to the cotton factories in the South. She took a job in a mill in Cottondale, Alabama. She watched children reach into the machinery with their hands and crawl under the machines to keep them oiled.

"Tiny babies of six years old with faces of sixty did an eight-hour shift for ten cents a day."

One day Mother Jones saw the body of an eleven-year-old girl whose scalp had been torn off when her hair was caught in a machine at the mill.

This time Mother Jones headed for New York City to stir up public pressure against the millowners by describing these sights to investors and stockholders. Again she won.

Mother Jones became embroiled in countless labor battles over the years, but her most frequent efforts were for coal miners and their families. Many of the workers were newly arrived immigrants, who had been promised free land if they went to work in the mines— a promise never kept, replaced instead by economic servitude from which there was no escape. Miners lived in company towns, in company houses, and bought overpriced food in company stores, using company credit which their wages could never possibly repay.

Mother Jones helped to organize the mine workers in Pennsylvania and West Virginia. The mineowners countered her efforts by blacklisting union members, evicting them, cutting off credit at company stores, and causing beatings and sometimes shootings.

Mother Jones redoubled her efforts.

In Arnot, Pennsylvania, when scabs were hired by the mineowners to break a five months' strike, Mother Jones organized a women's march on the minehead. The aim: to prevent the scabs from working, by blocking off access to the mine entrance. Their weapons: mops, brooms and pails of water, and, most effective of all, dishpans. By beating on these and yelling at the top of their lungs, the women scattered the mules that were used to haul the coal carts.

The women kept the strikebreakers from entering the mines for several days. At last, the company gave in. The victory served to confirm Mother Jones's conviction that "no strike has ever been won that didn't have the support of the women."

The owners had now marked Mother Jones as a troublemaker and tried to scare her off. In the state of West Virginia she was arrested and sentenced to twenty years' imprisonment by a state militia military court. She was only released as a result of a timely change in administration.

In Colorado, where she went when she was in her seventies, she was hunted by units of the state militia to prevent her from helping striking copper miners. When the militia finally caught her, she was imprisoned for over a month until public outrage forced the mineowners to let her go.

In 1914, the National Guard attacked a tent city

of miners near Ludlow, Colorado, killing four men, three women and eleven children. Mother Jones launched a nationwide campaign to raise funds to help the miners and their families. Public opinion swung to her side and the mineowners sat down to negotiate.

Mother Jones remained on call to aid strikers throughout her life. She was always ready to go wherever she was needed. In her eighties, she helped lead streetcar and garment strikes in New York. When she was over ninety she returned to West Virginia to lead a new generation of miners in the fight for their rights.

To millions of American working men and women, Mother Jones was the personification of *perseverance* in the face of adversity and harassment. Clarence Darrow praised her courage in these words:

> In all her career, Mother Jones never quailed or ran away. Her deep convictions and fearless soul always drew her to seek the spot where the fight was hottest and the danger greatest.

Men of goodwill in both North and South strove hard for many years to avoid war over the slavery issue. Lincoln himself believed up until the last minute that it was possible to work out an accommodation, a live-and-let-live national policy that would leave slavery intact in the Southern states and keep it from spreading. A key premise of this policy was the widespread belief that slaves were content with their lot, and that the slavery system provided protection and security for people who were unable to fend for themselves.

Two significant events destroyed that myth and helped to build public support for total abolition of slavery. One was the publication of Harriet Beecher

Stowe's *Uncle Tom's Cabin*. The other was the "Underground Railroad," a secret network of sympathizers who provided comfort and assistance for slaves who managed to escape from their owners and find their way to the Northern states.

The story of the Underground Railroad is not unlike that of the resistance fighters in Occupied France during World War II. Ordinary people of deep conviction and personal courage took substantial risks to rescue fellow human beings who needed help in their flight from bondage.

The risks increased with the passage of the Fugitive Slave Law of 1850, which made it a federal crime to help a runaway slave.

During the debate in Congress on the bill, one Southern senator claimed that over fifty thousand slaves had already run away to the North. This not only represented a huge financial loss to the Southern economy, of course, but it also contradicted the rosy picture of slave contentment that Southern spokesmen had attempted to portray.

Bounty hunters were organized in Southern states to search for escaped slaves. Wanted posters with large rewards were put up along known escape routes. Vigilante groups raided slave quarters in the south and policed slave gatherings to hunt for escapees, weapons and subversive abolitionist literature.

The biggest reward was on the head of Harriet Tubman, an ex-slave who had run away in 1849 when she learned that she was to be sold because of her owner's sagging finances. Physically deformed since her early teens, when she was struck in the head by a lead weight thrown by a white overseer, Harriet Tubman performed heavy field labor for many years. She had grown to believe that her only real choice in life was one between freedom and death. She made her choice to seek freedom, and one night headed north on foot, guided by the North Star and the mossy sides of trees. She walked from Dorchester County, Maryland, to Philadelphia, a distance of several hundred miles, where a Quaker woman helped her find work.

The following year, Harriet Tubman returned to Maryland and led other members of her family to freedom. After realizing what she was able to accomplish, she decided to become a regular "conductor" on the Underground Railroad.

In time, the reward for Harriet Tubman, dead or alive, reached $40,000, possibly the largest amount ever offered for a woman "outlaw." In all, she made nineteen trips into slave territory between 1850 and 1860, and led an estimated three hundred slaves to freedom, never losing one along the way.

Harriet Tubman often gave speeches before abolitionist meetings, describing slave life in the South. She helped John Brown plan his raid on the arsenal at Harpers Ferry, the spark that precipitated the attack on Fort Sumter four months later. Unlike others who dismissed Brown as a bungling zealot, Tubman understood that his self-sacrificing mission was intended to precipitate the armed conflict that she and he believed was necessary before slavery could be ended.

During Civil War combat, Harriet Tubman went to work behind enemy lines gathering military intelligence and planning raids by assault parties. She freed hundreds more slaves, and became their instructor and champion in helping them adjust to their new status.

Following the war, she turned her attention to the elderly ex-slaves who, disoriented by their change in status, required special understanding and attention.

Harriet Tubman's perseverance was legendary. She was often referred to as "Moses" and pictured as a giant, afraid of no one. Her strength, however, was not so much physical as intellectual and spiritual. Her success in spiriting slaves to freedom turned on her ability to outwit pursuers. She was well aware of the risk she was running—certain death by hanging if she was caught—and she took great pains to plan her operations with care.

Escapes usually began on a Saturday night, since slaves would not be counted again until Monday morning. Ms. Tubman used a biblical code system of her own to arrange meeting places, making references to passages which had meaning only to the initiated. She carried a pistol not for protection but to discourage the fainthearted from turning back when they became weary, thereby placing their traveling companions in jeopardy.

Sometimes she recruited people to follow her path and remove the Wanted posters for her current group of escaping slaves. She frequently dressed male slaves as women, to confound pursuers. Special precautions were required in crossing bridges and using public transportation, both easy marks for bounty hunters. On one occasion she switched her party from a northbound to a southbound platform at a depot to throw a slave-hunting patrol off the scent.

One day Harriet Tubman bought several live chickens to feed her band of escapees. Walking down the street, she spotted a relative of her former owner who she feared might recognize her. Without hesitation, she dumped her precious chickens onto the sidewalk, scattering them in all directions, and she and her wards escaped.

William H. Seward, former governor of New York and the first Republican United States senator from that state, was an admirer and a supporter of Harriet Tubman. When she needed a home for her aged parents after leading them to freedom, Seward helped her buy a small farm on the outskirts of his hometown, Auburn, New York, down the street from his own home. The dwelling is now preserved as a national shrine.

Seward was a militant abolitionist, whose strong views cost him the Republican presidential nomination in 1860 to the more moderate Abraham Lincoln of Illinois. Seward served in Lincoln's cabinet as secretary of state, and was marked for assassination along with Lincoln by John Wilkes Booth and his associates. He escaped with a bad wound.

In 1846, Seward's public career appeared to be at an end because of his stubborn perseverance in defending a black man who was an admitted murderer.

The defendant was William Freeman, son of a laundress in Auburn, who admitted killing the Van Nest family (friends and clients of Seward's) during a grisly nighttime assault with knife and hatchet.

Freeman had previously served a five-year prison term for horse stealing, for which he maintained his innocence. While in prison he was struck on the head by a prison guard using a heavy wooden club, and apparently had sustained permanent brain damage.

He explained his killing of the Van Nests as revenge for his unjust conviction for horse theft—

although they had had nothing to do with that case.

Seward was convinced that Freeman was mentally ill and did not have the capacity to understand the serious nature of what he had done. When the presiding judge assigned him to represent Freeman without fee, he felt it a matter of duty to accept.

The prosecution—and most residents of Auburn—had a different theory about the Van Nest murders. Seward had earlier advanced an insanity defense for a defendant charged with larceny during a trial in the very same Auburn courthouse, a few months before the Van Nest killings. After that attack someone remembered having seen Freeman in the courtroom. Freeman got the idea at the earlier trial, so the theory went, of feigning insanity in order to escape punishment for the Van Nest murders.

Feelings against Seward for his supposed role in encouraging Freeman's actions ran so high that when he returned to Auburn after being away for several weeks on another case, a mob met him at the railroad station and followed him home, threatening to harm him and his family if he defended Freeman.

The Freeman case was held in two stages: first a hearing to determine Freeman's mental capacity; then the trial for the actual crime. At the conclusion of the first hearing, the jury voted that Freeman could stand trial for the crime.

When the judge interrogated Freeman prior to the start of the second stage, he asked him if he had a lawyer. The defendant answered, "No."

"Do you know who that man is sitting next to you?" asked the judge, referring to Seward, who had just completed an eloquent plea on Freeman's behalf.

Freeman answered, "No."

Seward, overcome by emotion, got up and left the courtroom.

When he returned a short time later, the judge was in the process of asking lawyers in the courtroom: "Is there not anyone here who will serve as counsel for this defendant?"

Seward spoke up without hesitation: "I will, Your Honor."

The result of the trial was predictable: Freeman was found guilty on all counts.

Seward moved to set aside the verdict.

He appealed to the governor for a stay of execution.

He argued before the appellate division that the trial judge had ruled improperly on the issue of insanity.

Finally, just before the date set for execution, the appellate court ordered a new trial on the insanity defense.

The trial never came. Freeman died in jail of tuberculosis. An autopsy performed by a team of leading scientists revealed diseased and acutely damaged brain tissue, and concluded that the defendant in fact was incapable of normal behavior. Seward was vindicated.

During his summation, Seward had acknowledged that he was aware of the price he was paying for persevering in his defense of Freeman. He explained to the jury his obligation to the concept of justice. It was one of the most moving arguments in American legal annals:

> In due time, gentlemen of the Jury, when I shall have paid my debt to nature, my remains will rest here in your midst, with those of my kindred and neighbors.

It is very possible they may be unhonored, neglected, spurned.

But perhaps hence, when the passion and excitement which now agitates this community shall have passed away, some stranger, some lone exile, some Indian, some Negro, may erect over them an humble stone, and thereon this epitaph—

HE WAS FAITHFUL.

Seward's prediction became fact, except for one detail. When he died, it was the legal community itself that provided the tombstone that now stands over his grave, inscribed with the words he himself had chosen:

HE WAS FAITHFUL.

A young lawyer working on Wall Street during the 1950s used to take occasional lunch-hour walks over to the Fulton Fish Market. He ate fresh fish at Sloppy Louie's along with the waterfront workmen, and then made his way back to the office along different side streets, admiring the remaining groups of early nineteenth-century brick buildings which had witnessed the era when prows of sailing ships crowded along South Street as America's commerce passed through the port of New York.

As the years passed he watched with dismay as the groups of old buildings were razed, one after another, usually for no purpose other than to create parking lots. Soon there was only one complete group of early nineteenth-century buildings left: Schermerhorn Row on the south side of Fulton Street, built in 1802 across from the old Fulton Market.

He decided to try to do something to save the row.

He wrote an article suggesting that the buildings be used as a maritime museum, an urban version of Mystic Seaport. He persuaded a civic group to request a grant for a museum feasibility study. He drafted and introduced a maritime museum bill in the state legislature, which was passed and sent to the governor for signature, there to be met with strong opposition from a real-estate group headed by powerful banking interests led by the governor's own brother. Other opposition came from jealous competing groups with their own museum plans. But the lawyer kept pressing and the bill became law.

He recruited candidates for the museum's board of directors, cajoled the governor's staff to speed appointments, contributed money out of his pocket to help pay for a preliminary model of the proposed museum, and encouraged a bright advertising executive and his friends to start the museum idea on a shoestring.

Despite pressing professional obligations he was always on call to meet with city officials, testify at Board of Estimate and Planning Commission hearings, attend community meetings, and serve on working committees of the museum's board in order to help advance the project. On July 28, 1983, a gala opening ceremony was held for a new South Street Seaport Marketplace, with dozens of shops, a rebuilt market, and thousands of daily visitors, directly across Fulton Street from Schermerhorn Row, itself fully renovated as part of the development of the maritime museum complex.

More than thirty years had passed since the lawyer first visited Fulton Street during his lunch hours,

yet he was still at work—still as a volunteer—pushing
forward the maritime museum dream.

Perseverance.

Perseverance is not the same quality as commitment.
Commitment depends on our state of mind; perseverance depends on our fortitude in facing obstacles.

We must have sufficient commitment that others
cannot talk us out of what we are doing.

We must have sufficient perseverance that others
cannot prevent us from accomplishing what we are
doing.

> Commitment requires conviction.
> Perseverance requires courage.
> The mind plus the heart.
> Brains and guts.
> You need both.

Generosity

It is amazing how much you can get done if you
don't care who gets the credit.

—HAROLD WARP, sign in Pioneer
Village, Minden, Nebraska

In late December 1982, the board of directors of the
Boys Brotherhood Republic of New York held a brief
memorial service before their regular business session.
The service was in memory of a board member who had
died of a heart attack a few weeks before. His name was
Meyer Licht, probably known only to the handful of
people in that room and a few others in the neighborhood. For Meyer Licht was a modest, quiet man who
had given virtually all of his free time to BBR for over
twenty years. He was a product of the Lower East Side
neighborhood where BBR operated. His parents had
been beneficiaries of BBR's program to aid the elderly,
and his son was one of the club's alumni. He knew firsthand the value of the boys' club to poor youngsters.

BBR's Camp Wabenaki in Harriman State Park
was Meyer's particular turf. Every year he watched
over its operation, helping load the boys on buses, vis-

iting as often as he could, urging on the staff, counselors and campers to keep the place in shape for those to follow. Year after year, the camp received a 100 percent rating from state inspectors, largely because Meyer Licht cared.

At the memorial service, a prayer was read by Monsignor Harry J. Byrne, a fellow board member. Ralph Hitman, BBR's able and dedicated director, spoke quietly about Meyer's loyalty and kindness. Then David Paget, a former BBR student mayor (and now a successful lawyer and BBR board member) read, from the writings of the twelfth-century Hebrew scholar Maimonides, an essay on Charity, which had been a favorite of Meyer Licht's:

> There are eight degrees or steps in the duty of charity. The *first* and lowest degree is to give, but with reluctance or regret. This is the gift of the hand, but not of the heart.
>
> The *second* is, to give cheerfully, but not proportionately to the distress of the sufferer.
>
> The *third* is, to give cheerfully and proportionately, but not until solicited.
>
> The *fourth* is, to give cheerfully, proportionately, and even unsolicited; but to put it in the poor man's hand, thereby exciting in him the painful emotion of shame.
>
> The *fifth* is, to give charity in such a way that the distressed may receive the bounty, and know their benefactor, without their being known to him. Such was the conduct of some of our ancestors, who used to tie up money in the corners of their cloaks, so that the poor might take it unperceived.
>
> The *sixth,* which rises still higher is to know the objects of our bounty, but remain unknown to them.

Such was the conduct of those of our ancestors, who used to convey their charitable gifts into poor people's dwellings; taking care that their own persons and names should remain unknown.

The *seventh* is still more meritorious, namely to bestow charity in such a way that the benefactor may not know the relieved persons, nor they the name of their benefactors, as was done by our charitable forefathers during the existence of the Temple. For there was in that holy building a place called the Chamber of the Silent, wherein the good deposited secretly whatever their generous hearts suggested, and from which the poor were maintained with equal secrecy.

Lastly, the *eighth*, and the most meritorious of all, is to anticipate charity, by preventing poverty; namely, to assist the reduced fellowman, either by a considerable gift, or a loan of money, or by teaching him a trade, or by putting him in the way of business, so that he may earn an honest livelihood; and not be forced to the dreadful alternative of holding out his hand for charity. This is the highest step and the summit of charity's golden ladder.

The *eighth* degree of charity was the one practiced by Meyer Licht. In fact, it is the whole premise on which the Boys Brotherhood Republic was built, the very essence of unselfishness in helping others.

New York's Lower East Side slums changed San Francisco debutante Maude Younger into a laborite and woman suffragist. "I was on my way to Europe in 1901 when it began to happen," she explained to a *New York Times* reporter in the fall of 1919. "I'd been going abroad every summer since childhood, but this time I stopped off in New York to spend a week at the College

Settlement to see tenement conditions. I stayed five years. During that time I grew to know the wage-earning woman and her problems far better than I had ever known anything else, and everything I learned was one more argument for suffrage."

Described by a contemporary as "a singularly warm and arresting personality, vitally interested in the lives of others," Maude Younger became one with the weariest toilers in the ranks. She went to work as a waitress for a restaurant chain in New York, joined the local union, then returned to San Francisco and repeated the experience there. Since there was no union in her home city, she organized one and was elected its first president.

"A trade unionist—of course I am," she said. "First, last and all the time. How else strike at the roots of the evils undermining the moral and physical health of women? How else grapple with the complex problems of employment, overemployment and unemployment, alike resulting in discouraged, undernourished bodies, too tired to resist the onslaughts of disease and crime?"

She was soon in the forefront of the successful drive for an eight-hour workday for women. She also campaigned for approval of women's suffrage for state elections, stumping throughout California and organizing a working women's association to campaign for its adoption.

It was only a matter of time before Maude Younger became active in the national drive for the women's vote in federal elections. She was the chief lobbyist in Washington during the last years of the fight, and directed that effort until its final success.

During the 1911 Labor Day parade, Ms. Younger caused a stir by personally driving a team of six horses pulling the suffrage float down Market Street—a difficult feat for a man.

The following year she returned to New York to support the ILGWU strike against subcontracting of needlework to sweatshops. She marched on picket lines from dawn until night, then appeared at night court to help provide bail for pickets who had been arrested.

Grace Dodge was the wealthy daughter of the man who founded Phelps Dodge Corporation. She was educated by private tutors. At the age of eighteen she began teaching Sunday-school classes. One day at Sunday school, she met a worker from a silk factory who was exactly her age. They talked for a while, and Ms. Dodge asked her new friend if she would be willing to invite a group of factory girls to meet on a weekly basis. This discussion group soon grew into a national association of working girls, and worked to establish education programs for young women from lower-income families.

Responding to the need for better-trained teachers in the city's public schools, the "Industrial Education Association" began to concentrate on the recruitment and training of teachers. Grace Dodge worked to establish a New York College for the Training of Teachers, which soon became Teachers College, chartered by the state of New York, and today affiliated with Columbia University.

From the start, Grace Dodge made it a practice to work the same hours as other working women and limited herself to one two-week vacation each year. Her entire life was spent helping others who had been denied the advantages she had received, never asking anything in return.

In 1896, Marian MacDowell purchased a sixty-acre farm near Peterborough, New Hampshire, and built a secluded log studio in the woods behind the farmhouse so that her composer husband could write music without interruption. Edward MacDowell, the first serious American composer to win world fame, died shortly afterward, and his widow decided to create a full-scale artists' retreat in his memory.

Mrs. MacDowell was a gifted pianist and spent months on the road giving recitals and lectures to raise money to buy more land and build more studios. The result was The MacDowell Colony, which provides creative artists a tranquil haven where they can work without interruption, offering studios and living accommodations at nominal cost.

Among the authors and composers who benefited from Mrs. MacDowell's efforts were Willa Cather, Stephen Vincent Benét, Aaron Copland and Thornton Wilder. Although Marian MacDowell has now been dead many years, new generations of serious artists are still doing creative work in the New Hampshire hill studios she personally raised the money to build.

Literary critic Alexander Woollcott (whose irascible wit was caricatured as Sheridan Whiteside in *The Man Who Came to Dinner*) went out of his way to help undiscovered playwrights and authors. Once Woollcott was having lunch with Laurence Stallings, co-author (with Maxwell Anderson) of a new play entitled *What Price Glory?*, which Woollcott had read and liked. Broadway producer Arthur Hopkins stopped by their table and Woollcott introduced the young playwright to Hopkins; then he turned to Stallings and commented acidly that Hopkins "never read" plays since he was a producer. Rising to the bait, Hopkins demanded the right to read Stallings's manuscript. *What Price Glory?* became the most popular war play of the 1920s.

Woollcott was always on the lookout for opportunities to help talented young people, with no reward except the satisfaction of seeing their talent recognized. It was he who brought Paul Robeson together with Jerome Kern, resulting in *Show Boat,* and who suggested to Harold Ross that the vaudevillian Will Rogers be invited to write humor for *Judge* magazine. He also was credited with discovering Fred Astaire and encouraging vaudeville stage managers to give him a try.

Woollcott had a reputation for being a "soft touch" whenever anyone needed a loan. He was particularly generous to students. Once he underwrote a medical student who had come from Denmark as a cabin boy, so he would be free to give full time to his studies. In that case, Woollcott's reward was being best man at the young doctor's wedding, and godfather to his first child.

Isaac Stern is one of the world's great virtuoso violinists. He plays more than a hundred concerts each season, traveling to all parts of the globe. He is known and hailed from France to China, and he is a folk hero in Israel.

His musical gift is his instinctive ability to perceive music "from the inside" and to perform with exquisite tone, gesture and expression.

Years ago Stern discovered the satisfaction of giving time and energy to public service when he helped organize a citizens committee to save Carnegie Hall in New York City from demolition. That was in 1960. To consolidate the committee's initial success, he consented to serve as president of the Carnegie Hall Corporation to help ensure its economic health. He contributed thousands of hours as president and performed at numerous benefits to raise needed funds.

Stern had reached the top of his field by the time he was fifty. He received accolades that were dizzying. He was accepted into the small group of international celebrities in politics and the arts. He might easily have settled for that and nothing more. But he did not. The reason:

> You have to give some of it back.
> You can't just *take* all the time;
> It's simply not right.

Isaac Stern gave it back by serving as mentor to a series of talented young people who were just starting out. He first heard Pinchas Zukerman play the violin on a visit to Israel when Pinchas was only nine. Stern tracked him down on a return trip (Pinchas was now thirteen) and persuaded a foundation to finance the boy's way to New York for advanced study.

Stern repeated his quiet encouragement with violinists Itzhak Perlman, Miriam Fried, Shlomo Mintz and Sergiu Luca, pianist Yefim Bronfman, and cellist Yo-Yo Ma. To all he gave advice and guidance, plus practical help in finding financial support. Most important of all, he encouraged and nurtured that precious element: self-confidence.

Despite Stern's own considerable personal achieve-

ments, his greatest fulfillment has come from helping
his community and the young people just starting out:

> I look at colleagues and friends who are just musi-
> cians and think, *"That's* the beginning and end of
> everything in life?"

Isaac Stern knows better.

Envy and pride are part of the human baggage we all
carry with us. These qualities, fed by insecurity, are always getting in our way. They cause bitterness, dissat-
isfaction and, worst of all, the desire to destroy the
achievements of others. Many people, when they discover a contemporary getting ahead, go out of their
way to bad-mouth him or her, or throw roadblocks
across the path.

It is a rare person who can reach out a helping
hand to a talented contemporary. English writer and
editor Ford Madox Ford was such a person—a man of
enormous generosity who used his role as editor to fos-
ter unrecognized gifted writers.

Ford Madox Ford was raised by his maternal
grandfather, Ford Madox Brown, a leading painter of
the Victorian era. Brown was a contemporary of
Browning, Carlyle, Gladstone, Ruskin and Tennyson
and despised their vanity and jealousies. His grandfather told Ford:

> Beggar yourself rather than refuse assistance to
> anyone whose genius you think shows promise of being
> greater than your own.

Although a considerable literary talent in his own
right, Ford Madox Ford's principal achievement was

encouraging other writers. At first, Ford concentrated on writing letters of praise and constructive criticism—particularly to Joseph Conrad, John Galsworthy and H. G. Wells. Then in 1908, he founded the *English Review*, a literary magazine designed expressly to provide an outlet for unknown writers, including work by D. H. Lawrence, Wyndham Lewis and Ezra Pound. In true tradition, the literary establishment was soon attacking Ford and his magazine for poor taste and poor judgment.

Following World War I, Ford Madox Ford moved to Paris, where he helped an emerging new generation of writers, including Ernest Hemingway, Jean Rhys and Katherine Anne Porter. He published these writers in a literary magazine, *Transatlantic Review*, and gave them personal editorial critiques and advice. For his pains Ford learned the lesson of ingratitude.

Hemingway lampooned him in *The Sun Also Rises* and *A Moveable Feast*. Rhys demeaned him in *Postures*. Only one of his beneficiaries, Katherine Anne Porter, recognized the injustice of these reactions to Ford's generosity:

> I have never seen an essay or article about him signed by any of these discoveries of his. I can make nothing of this, except that I have learned that most human beings—and I suppose that artists are that, after all—suffer some blow to their self-esteem in being helped, and develop the cancer of ingratitude. As if, somehow, they can, by denying their debt, or ignoring it, wipe it out altogether.

In his later years, Ford Madox Ford spent much of his time in the United States. He enjoyed some recognition as a literary figure, but little practical help. He lived modestly in a single room, wore old clothes and was forced to watch his pennies closely. When he died in 1939, there were some who recognized how much Ford had meant in the lives of others. Wrote Sherwood Anderson:

> Ford was a rich man. He was rich in a way we would all secretly like to be rich. He was rich in good work done, in self-respect.

Mark Twain observed, with his exceptional insight into human nature:

> If you pick up a starving dog, and make him prosperous, he will not bite you. That is the principal difference between dog and man.

It is an unfortunate truth that generosity is rarely followed by gratitude. Some beneficiaries will give lip service, maybe, but more often they feel a resentment that the donor was not even *more* generous. This truth holds whether the gift is money, a helping hand or personal service. We are peculiar creatures.

Whenever you enter upon a generous course of action never do so in the expectation of recognition and thanks. The action itself must be its own reward—the sense of having done something for another human being that was out of the ordinary.

Maimonides learned that lesson, almost a thousand years ago. If we can only remember the eight degrees of charity, there are no limits to the service we can render to others.

Building Your Resources

C H A P T E R   *7*

Follow Your Instincts

> That everyone shall exert himself in that state of
> life in which he is placed, to practice true human-
> ity toward his fellow men—on that depends the
> future of mankind.
>
> —DR. ALBERT SCHWEITZER

Late one afternoon in September 1915, Dr. Albert
Schweitzer was sitting on the deck of a small steamboat
making its way up the Ogooué River in central Africa.
Schweitzer, who at forty had already achieved a remarkable record as a scholar and musician, was at the
threshold of his most important lifework—bringing
medical services to the native population in French
Equatorial Africa.

Sunset was approaching. The boat had slowed
down and was moving cautiously through a herd of
hippopotami wallowing in the river. As Schweitzer
watched the evasive actions of the ship's captain to
avoid hitting the animals, he came to a profound realization—the captain personified the highest ethical
principle: reverence for the life of other creatures.

For years Dr. Schweitzer had been searching for

the key ethic in the modern world. Here on a muddy
river in Africa he found it—"Reverence for life":

> The iron door had yielded, the path in the thicket
> had become visible [he wrote later]. Now I had my way
> to the idea in which world—and life—affirmation and
> ethics are contained side by side!

Dr. Schweitzer summarized his discovery in these
words:

> A man is ethical only when life, as such, is sacred
> to him, that of plants and animals as that of his fellow
> men, and when he devotes himself helpfully to all life
> that is in need of help.

It is not enough for the scholar to devote himself to science alone, **Dr.** Schweitzer wrote, even if his work is
useful to the community. It is not enough for the artist
to live only for his art, even if it is inspirational to
others. It is not enough for the businessman to serve
the public through the honest and efficient conduct of
his business affairs.

> It demands from all that they should sacrifice a
> portion of their own lives for others.

It is fashionable in today's medical world to criticize
Schweitzer and his treatment methods. But few of his
critics can match his record of putting his ideals into
practice through personal service. Most of those who
criticize Schweitzer do so from the comfortable pre-
cincts of well-endowed hospitals and academic institutions. There is not much criticism from the jungle.

Schweitzer first developed his plan to spend most
of his life in public service when he was still a university student.

While at the university and enjoying the happiness of being able to study and even to produce some results in science and art, I could not help thinking continually of others who were denied that happiness by their material circumstances or their health.

Then one brilliant summer morning at Günsbach, during the Whitsuntide holidays—it was in 1896— there came to me, as I awoke, the thought that I must not accept this happiness as a matter of course, but must give something in return for it.

Proceeding to think the matter out at once with calm deliberation, while the birds were singing outside, I settled with myself before I got up that I would consider myself justified in living till I was thirty for science and art, in order to devote myself from that time forward to the direct service of humanity.

Schweitzer's accomplishments in science and art by the time he was thirty were more than most people achieve in a lifetime. He was an expert musician at piano and organ. He published a biography of Johann Sebastian Bach as well as a volume of Bach's organ music. He wrote several theological works and had already been appointed principal of the Theological College of Saint Thomas at the University of Strasbourg.

Friday the thirteenth was the critical turning point in Schweitzer's career. On that date in October 1905, he sent off letters to his parents and friends telling them that he intended to begin the study of medicine and planned to spend the rest of his life in service to humanity. Well-meaning friends told him he was burying his talent. His music teacher said it was like a general going into the firing line. But he persisted.

For seven years Schweitzer studied medicine, gaining his degree in 1913. In the interim he married

the daughter of a historian in Strasbourg, who studied
to be a nurse so she could assist her husband in Africa.

The Paris Missionary Society sent Schweitzer and
his wife to establish a hospital at an outpost in the
African jungle at Lambaréné. The climate was op-
pressive—hot days, clammy nights, seasonal down-
pours of rain. Native diseases were rife: leprosy,
dysentery, elephantiasis, malaria, yellow fever, sleeping sickness.

With only an old chicken coop to start, Dr.
Schweitzer began to build a jungle hospital that grew
to contain more than 70 buildings with 350 beds, and a
separate leper colony for 200 patients. The hospital
compound was staffed by five unpaid physicians, seven
nurses and thirteen volunteer aides.

Dr. Schweitzer's Lambaréné hospital was more
native village than conventional institution, to give
the patients a feeling of confidence and security. It at-
tracted thousands of natives seeking medical treatment. Dr. Schweitzer not only ministered to the
patients' physical well-being, but also to their spiritual
side, through sermons and example. From all corners
of the world people came to study his methods and be
inspired by his example. It was almost an anticlimax
when he was awarded the Nobel Peace Prize, for his
name had become synonymous with brotherly love.

One day in 1874, a prosperous Iowa farmer named
Lorenzo Coffin witnessed the maiming of a railroad
brakeman. The train on which he was riding had
stopped to pick up a freight car, and as the train
backed up to hook the coupling, the brakeman's hand
was caught in the mechanism and two of his fingers

were cut off. Mr. Coffin asked how the accident had happened, and learned that the brakeman had been dropping a pin between two iron loops as the car couplers came together. A slight miscalculation had caused a disabling injury he would carry the rest of his life.

Coffin began asking more questions. He learned that twenty to thirty thousand brakemen were maimed or killed each year because of the absence of railroad safety devices. He also learned that an automatic coupler had been developed but the railroads did not want to bear the added expense. Labor was cheap and the railroad owners had no liability for injuries caused by the employee's own "fault."

Coffin also discovered that brakemen had to ride on top of freight trains in order to set the hand brakes to slow or stop the trains, even though air brakes existed which permitted an engineer to stop the freight train from inside the locomotive.

Lorenzo Coffin got his dander up. Despite imposing opposition, he launched his own one-man crusade to protect railroad brakemen against senseless injury.

Coffin talked to anyone who would listen—newspapermen, legislators, civic groups. Most of them shrugged him off. By 1883, nine years after the brakeman's accident, Coffin got himself appointed Railroad Commissioner for the state of Iowa. He wrote railroad executives on his official letterhead haranguing them to install safety equipment. He arranged for test demonstrations of air brakes to prove that they worked.

He organized a lobbying campaign in Congress, where he was soon called the "Air-Brake Fanatic." He built grass-roots support in all parts of the country.

Finally in 1893, after nineteen years of his persistent pressure, Congress passed legislation mandating all railroads to install both air brakes and automatic couplers. At the bill-signing ceremony, President Benjamin Harrison presented Lorenzo Coffin the pen used to sign the legislation into law.

During the first year after enactment of the Coffin legislation, casualties among railroad trainmen were cut in half.

Wendell Phillips was a product of the nearest thing there is to a New England aristocracy. His father was a leading lawyer and the first mayor of the city of Boston. Wendell attended Boston Public Latin School, Harvard College and Harvard Law School. A successful career at the bar seemed certain.

Then came the day when Wendell Phillips looked out of his law office window and observed a mob attacking the office of abolitionist William Lloyd Garrison across the street. As he watched, he saw the mob drag Garrison from his office at the end of a rope. He rushed to the street, where he recognized the commander of the local militia in the crowd. Phillips asked why the mayor had not called out the troops. The colonel smiled, telling Phillips most of the militia were members of the mob. Phillips was aghast. Garrison was lodged in the Boston jail for his safety.

One of those who had been driven into the streets by the mob was Ann Terry Greene whom Phillips met and married soon thereafter.

The mob's treatment of Garrison outraged Phillips, and his involvement with the antislavery movement escalated rapidly. On December 8, 1837, he attended a protest meeting at Faneuil Hall called to consider resolutions condemning the murder of the editor of an antislavery journal in Alton, Illinois. Mobs had destroyed the journal's press three times before, but on the fourth occasion of mob violence the editor attempted to stop the destruction and was killed. Feelings ran high.

During the meeting, the Massachusetts attorney general came forward and mounted the platform. He argued against the protest resolutions, saying that abolitionists were fools and that the mob in Illinois was simply following the tradition of those who had dumped tea into Boston Harbor.

Phillips rose to respond. The eloquent and moving speech he delivered produced immediate passage of the resolutions. At that instant his future changed. Many of those who heard him in Faneuil Hall remembered his performance years later as one of the thrilling experiences of their lives.

Over the next twenty-five years, Wendell Phillips became the most powerful public orator in the abolitionist cause. Probably more than any other single person, Phillips built up the public pressure that led to the eventual signing of the Emancipation Proclamation.

After emancipation, Phillips's awareness of the plight of former slaves caused him to crusade for free land, free education and the right to vote.

In later years, Phillips turned his attention to better conditions for working men and women. He supported the eight-hour day and worker cooperatives, views regarded by some of his contemporaries as dangerous radicalism.

Wendell Phillips kept up his service to public

causes for almost fifty years. His last triumph was a
Phi Beta Kappa oration given at Harvard College, his
alma mater, in 1881, the year Phillips turned seventy.
He criticized the institution "as that Alpine height of
intellectual indifference." The title of his oration was
"The Scholar in a Republic." Phillips said that the
duty of intellectuals in a republic was to agitate on behalf of the great social issues of the day:

> Trust the people—the wise and the ignorant, the
> good and the bad—with the gravest questions, and in
> the end you educate the race. At the same time you se-
> cure, not perfect institutions, not necessarily good
> ones, but the best institutions possible while human
> nature is the basis and the only material to build with.

Lillian Wald came from a prosperous upstate New
York family. Her father ran a successful optical goods
business in Rochester, and she had every advantage a
young woman could ask for. But she was not happy
with her comfortable existence. One day a trained
nurse came to the house to care for her older sister, who
was ill. For Lillian, the nurse represented everything
noble and humanitarian, and she knew that she had to
make nursing her life's work.

In 1889, Lillian Wald enrolled in a school of nursing in New York City, then continued on to medical
school. While she was still at medical school, Lillian
was asked to organize classes in home hygiene for immigrant families on the Lower East Side. One day a
child came to one of her classes and said her mother
was very sick. Ms. Wald followed the child to a gloomy
tenement apartment where she found a desperately
sick woman who had not received any help for days.

The experience moved her deeply. Something was terribly wrong and she must do something about it.

Lillian Wald evolved a plan: She would live among people who most needed help and provide them direct, easy access to professional nursing service. Accompanied by a friend from the training school, Mary Brewster, she rented a tenement apartment on Jefferson Street and offered to supply nursing service to her neighbors on a nominal pay-what-you-can basis. Lillian Wald had taken the first step toward what was to become the Visiting Nurse Service.

Soon Lillian Wald and her friend had more patients than they could handle alone. She decided to raise funds to hire more nurses so the service could be enlarged. Her appeal was heartfelt and convincing, and Mrs. Solomon Loeb and her son-in-law, banker Jacob Schiff, agreed to help her establish an expanded visiting nurse service at 265 Henry Street on Manhattan's Lower East Side. The program grew rapidly and so did the need for services.

The Henry Street facility was soon turned into a full settlement house. It provided civic, educational, social and philanthropic services for the community, in addition to the visiting nurse service, now staffed by more than ninety professionally trained nurses making 200,000 home visits a year.

Meanwhile Lillian Wald saw the need to supplement direct public-health activities with a range of other services, and campaigned for the first public-school nursing program and the first full department of nursing and health for teacher training. She persuaded President Theodore Roosevelt to establish the first United States Children's Bureau in 1908.

Ms. Wald led campaigns to combat tuberculosis, to create more parks and playgrounds, to improve housing. She never rested. One well-to-do gentleman complained: "It costs five thousand dollars to sit next to her at dinner."

Stephen P. Duggan, Jr., was a partner in a Wall Street law firm for most of his professional career. His wife, Beatrice Abbott Duggan, appeared to be like any other homemaker, mother and grandmother. The Duggans had full opportunity to indulge in the material trappings of success—winter vacations in Florida or the Caribbean, country-club life, world travel.

But they simply were not able to spend their time and energies on such pleasures. Stephen Duggan was the son of a pioneering educator, one of the original founders of the Institute of International Education and a man of high ethical standards. Beatrice Abbott Duggan was the granddaughter of a leading cleric, Lyman Abbott, who had taken over Henry Ward Beecher's congregation after Beecher's disgrace and removal as rector of Plymouth Church in Brooklyn, New York. Lyman Abbott had founded *The Outlook*, an independent journal whose board of editors included former President Theodore Roosevelt. Mr. and Mrs. Duggan thus combined traditions of service and personal ethics that made it impossible for them to lead a sybaritic life.

They both gave time to good works (he to the Institute of International Education; she to Young Audiences), and worked hard at raising their family of three sons and a daughter in the same ethical tradition they had known.

One day the Duggans were drawn into a fight with the power company, when the Consolidated Edison Company of New York (Con Ed) tried to build a pumped-storage power plant in Storm King Mountain, the northern gateway to the Hudson Highlands, next door to Mrs. Duggan's family home.

The Duggans joined their neighbors in Cornwall, New York, to form a local citizens committee to challenge the pumped-storage permit granted to Con Ed by the Federal Power Commission. They went to court. Their case was argued by Lloyd K. Garrison (grandson of the abolitionist leader whose mistreatment had so aroused Wendell Phillips). The Second United States Court of Appeals—second only to the United States Supreme Court in its importance in federal jurisprudence—handed down a landmark opinion in what has come to be known as the *Scenic Hudson Preservation Conference* case, which opened the doors of federal courthouses to environmental protection cases for the first time. The court ordered the Federal Power Commission to give more attention to the public's interest in natural resources, and directed it to reconsider Con Ed's storage-plant license application.

This David-and-Goliath victory by a small group of citizens fighting a giant public utility became a rallying point for citizen committees. Local conservation groups around the country started asking the Scenic Hudson volunteers for advice and assistance in their own environmental battles.

Realizing that there were environmental battles to be fought across the nation—not just in the Hudson Highlands—the Duggans responded to the calls for help.

Stephen Duggan created a brand-new national citizen action organization, the Natural Resources Defense Council (NRDC); and recruited a highly motivated, able staff of young lawyers and scientists who were good enough to take on legal environmental battles anywhere and be the match for any lawyers the industrial polluters might hire.

For ten full years Stephen Duggan gave half of his working time to NRDC environmental battles to protect air, water, fish and wildlife, natural beauty and wilderness areas in all parts of the country—wherever there was need. NRDC grew into one of the foremost public-interest law offices in the country, and Stephen Duggan set a standard of integrity and commitment that was reflected in the entire organization.

Besides working with her husband in NRDC fund raising, Mrs. Duggan concentrated her attention on *international* environmental matters. She worked with United Nations committees; helped organize international conferences to raise the visibility of environmental concerns, especially in third world countries; opened channels of communication to developing nations to help them learn preventive measures in time to prevent or reduce the impact of industrialization.

In 1981, after ten years of intense effort, the Duggans both retired from active leadership of NRDC. They could look with satisfaction on a record of building a skilled organization of dedicated young professionals, scores of environmental victories, and a heightened awareness of our fragile environment around the world. It was fitting that their years of totally volunteer service should be honored by the establishment of a Duggan Fellowship, funded by gifts from friends and colleagues, to bring environmentalists from third world countries to the United States to work with NRDC and other organizations to learn how to identify and fight environmental threats to their own countries.

Albert Schweitzer recognized that far more people are idealists than will admit it:

> Just as the water of the streams we see is small in amount compared to that which flows underground, so the idealism which becomes visible is small in amount compared with what men and women bear locked in their hearts, unreleased or scarcely released. To unbind what is bound, to bring the underground waters to the surface: mankind is waiting and longing for such as can do that.

It is an odd quirk that makes us repress our idealism. We are embarrassed by good instincts and often go to great lengths to pretend to be hard-boiled and cynical when in reality we have a strong underlying desire to be good and to do good.

Idealism is nothing to be ashamed of. It is a noble attribute of tremendous force which can move mountains of indifference. Schweitzer, Coffin, Phillips, Wald, the Duggans were all idealists—who achieved monumental results simply by following their instincts.

Enlist Strong Teammates

One chops the wood; the other does the grunting.

—Ancient Hebrew proverb

Jane Addams grew up in a well-to-do Illinois family. She traveled and studied extensively after graduation from college and was headed for the life of a dilettante. But she had a secret dream. She visualized a group residence in an urban slum neighborhood which would study human needs firsthand and find causes and solutions. Her idea seemed fated to end as a daydream.

One day, while watching a bullfight in Madrid, Jane became angry at herself for her procrastination. She told her traveling companion, Ellen Gates Starr, her plan. Ellen was enthusiastic and offered to join her in the experiment. The two young women began to lay plans.

The first step was to visit the East End Settlement in London, started in 1884 by a group of Oxford undergraduates, to learn its operations. Then Addams and

Starr went to Chicago to look for a site for their experiment. They found a decaying mansion in the
crowded nineteenth ward which was jammed with immigrants living in cheap housing with inadequate mu-
nicipal services.

In September 1889, Jane Addams and Ellen Starr
opened the doors of Hull House. They were to live and
work there as a team for over forty years. It became the
banner settlement house in the nation. Within four
years, Hull House was operating over forty different
activities, ranging from a day nursery, a gymnasium, a
dispensary, a playground, cooking and sewing courses,
and a cooperative boardinghouse for working girls, to a
center for art, theater and music instruction. Two
thousand people a week used the building's facilities.

When it became apparent that a neighborhood
service center could not solve all the human problems
and needs in the nineteenth ward, Jane Addams and
Ellen Starr began organizing efforts to reform and improve working and living conditions. Hull House became the nerve center for pressure groups lobbying for
passage of Illinois' first factory inspection law, soon
followed by the battles for child-labor laws, restrictions
on working hours for women, protection of immigrants, compulsory school attendance, industrial
safety and labor-union recognition. At the same time,
Hull House pressed for the establishment of the nation's first juvenile court, which happened in 1899.

Jane Addams depended on the support of Ellen
Starr and that of an increasing number of other talented colleagues in these efforts, but she was the main
energizer, and with this support her capacity for leadership extended well beyond the immediate goals of

Hull House itself. She was an advocate of free speech and helped found the American Civil Liberties Union. She was a supporter of the trade-union movement, and urged adequate wages to provide family strength and stability. Her outspoken views on these subjects caused many people to regard her as dangerous. In later years Jane Addams became the target of attacks by so-called patriotic organizations for her "radical" ideas, which only strengthened her commitment to the principles she and her teammates had brought so close to full realization.

One of the alumni of Hull House was Benjamin David Goodman, one of eleven children born to an impoverished tailor and his wife who had emigrated from Eastern Europe. When the local synagogue offered to lend musical instruments to children so they could take music lessons, three of the Goodman boys were sent over to enroll. The oldest and strongest of the boys was handed a tuba; the middle-sized one, a trumpet; while Benjamin, the smallest, was given a clarinet. Soon he was doing so well he was sent over to Hull House to receive private lessons from a volunteer instructor from the Chicago Symphony Orchestra.

At thirteen, Benny Goodman received his first union card; at fourteen he left school to play in a band at a Chicago dance hall. By the time he was twenty-four, Benny Goodman had come to the attention of jazz critic John Hammond, who assisted him in organizing a group of other talented musicians to make a series of records for sale in England. With Hammond's help, Goodman formed his first permanent band, and with it came the dawn of the era of swing.

Out of this process came a simple example of teamwork which would, at a single stroke, destroy racial barriers that had for decades separated white and black musicians. Benny Goodman put together his first trio to give a public performance on Easter Sunday, 1936. Onstage sat a black musician—pianist Teddy Wilson—playing side by side with two white musicians, Goodman on clarinet and Gene Krupa on drums. It was the first time musicians of both races had ever performed together in public. The group soon expanded with the addition of Lionel Hampton, noted black xylophone player. From that time forward, the only question that mattered was the performers' ability to play.

The "King of Swing" had taught America that ability, not race, was the hallmark of American jazz.

In August 1899, Katherine Pettit and May Stone rode forty-five miles in a wagon over wood trails and rocky creek beds to the small town of Hazard, Kentucky, to organize a homemakers' "camp meeting." Both women had been active in the Federation of Women's Clubs which had received a letter from a clergyman in the Hazard community asking for homemaking help for his mountaineering families.

Katherine Pettit was already familiar with life on the Cumberland plateau in eastern Kentucky, which she had visited for five summers. She had gotten into the habit of taking along flower seeds and pictures each year to share with the women whose hard lives she had come to respect and admire. Now she persuaded May Stone to join her in establishing a formal summer training center for homemakers.

When the two young women arrived at Hazard, they set up a gaily trimmed tent and started to play games and tell stories to the curious children. Before long, mothers joined the group. Soon they were baking bread and beating biscuits, making cottage cheese, and preparing meat and vegetables to be nutritious and appetizing. Pettit and Stone taught sewing, songs and hygienic practices. When the first year's experimental camp meeting ended, a hundred people gathered around a bonfire to sing farewell to their visitors.

The following summer, the two young women came back and repeated the camp meeting, and did it again the next year as well. Each season was longer than the one before. It became clear that a permanent institution was needed.

The two women set out to create a mountain version of Hull House, the pioneering settlement in Chicago. Despite fire and other misfortune, by 1911 the Hindaman Settlement School was in full operation, with two hundred students and a resident staff of thirteen. Attention turned to crafts and other manual skills, in addition to domestic and health education, to help provide an income base for the mountain residents.

A friend of Katherine Pettit's from Lexington, Linda Neville, visited the school and learned about the problem of trachoma, a contagious eye disease, which was widespread in the mountains at the time and often led to blindness. She offered to help, and eventually escorted more than three thousand patients to Lexington for treatment. When she imported a Lexington specialist to the Hindaman School to conduct a series of clinics, the local residents insisted on paying for his services—in chickens, eggs, apples and buckets of honey.

In 1913, with the Hindaman School well launched with May Stone in charge, Katherine Pettit enlisted a new teammate, Ethel de Long, and headed for another mountain community, Pine Mountain, to start a new settlement school. To do this meant clearing virgin forest and transporting logs by oxen forty miles to a sawmill. At the new school Pettit and De Long established an extension program to serve isolated one-room schools; provide health centers; set up trachoma, hookworm and dental clinics; and run farmers' institutes to encourage the development of marketable commodities. To preserve the economic independence of the mountain people, Katherine Pettit encouraged home dyeing and handweaving along with ballad singing and folk dancing.

Shortly before she died in 1936, Katherine Pettit wrote to a friend:

> This has been a glorious world to work in, I am eager to see what the next will be.

Her teammates had helped make it so.

Women's suffrage was one of the most extraordinary civic achievements in American history. Its goal was not merely votes for women, but also the elimination of many inequities in laws governing the ownership of property, the right of a wife to her own earnings, divorce laws and other irrational legal distinctions. While changes in statutory law could be effected through state legislatures, winning the vote in federal elections required a United States constitutional amendment, and that meant a national effort with extensive planning, work, funds and commitment.

Much of the success of the movement can be attributed to the friendship and teamwork of two women: Elizabeth Cady Stanton and Susan B. Anthony.

Elizabeth Cady was born in 1815 in Johnstown, New York. Her lawyer father served in the state legislature, in Congress and as a judge of the state Supreme Court. As a child, Elizabeth spent time in her father's law office, where she not only learned basic legal principles, but also came to know the legal problems of married women who were deprived of their property or their children under the existing law. When her only brother died, she decided to prove to her father that a daughter was every bit as valuable as a son. She enrolled in a course of intensive study, including Greek and Latin, subjects not usually open to women. She became competitive in horsemanship, chess and other "masculine" games and sports.

One day Elizabeth Cady joined the antislavery movement, where she met and married Henry Brewster Stanton, one of the leading speakers against slavery. (Her one condition to the marriage ceremony was that the word "obey" be omitted.) After the wedding, she and her husband attended the world's first antislavery convention in London, and discovered that women were not permitted to serve as delegates. She was enraged. So was another excluded delegate whom she met there, Lucretia Mott. (See Chapter 9.)

The Stantons settled in Seneca Falls, New York, where Mr. Stanton practiced law and was elected to the State Senate. Mrs. Stanton seized the opportunity to start lobbying with other legislators for equal property rights for married women.

In July 1848, Elizabeth Stanton met with Lucretia Mott to plan a conference on women's rights to be held in Seneca Falls. Mrs. Stanton drafted a "declaration of sentiments" based on the Declaration of Independence. The statement declared that all *men and women* are created equal, and enumerated eighteen legal grievances of women, including denial of the right to vote. The convention was a success and led to a series of such conventions over the ensuing years. The right to vote became the rallying cry for every women's rights meeting.

In 1851, Susan B. Anthony visited Seneca Falls to attend an antislavery meeting, and met Elizabeth Cady Stanton for the first time. They became immediate friends. Mrs. Stanton persuaded Miss Anthony that the ballot for women was essential and worth fighting for. They agreed to work together.

The teamwork between Stanton and Anthony combined two quite different talents for maximum effect. Ms. Anthony was an organizer with a zest for campaigning on the road; Mrs. Stanton was a writer and an eloquent speaker, with family obligations that kept her at home. Anthony became the traveling member of the team, while Stanton wrote speeches, leaflets and resolutions. The overall strategy was developed by the two women jointly:

> Night after night by an old-fashioned fireplace, we plotted and planned the coming agitation.

Mrs. Stanton wrote articles on women's rights for the *New York Tribune.* She sent letters to all parts of the country organizing the women's rights movement. Ms. Anthony meanwhile was on the road, attending meetings, urging all who would listen to give women an equal voice in the election of their representatives.

When the Civil War came, both women turned their efforts to the immediate abolition of slavery. Then, when the war came to an end, they returned to the goal of women's rights.

Their impact was widespread—in Kansas, in the Far West, at the Philadelphia Centennial Exposition of 1876. A United States senator from California was persuaded to introduce the necessary constitutional amendment for women's suffrage. The amendment was reintroduced in every succeeding Congress until it finally passed.

Anthony and Stanton decided to make legal tests of unfair restrictions in the law. Mrs. Stanton ran for Congress in 1866 to establish women's constitutional right to seek public office (she was defeated). Susan Anthony registered to vote in 1872, was arrested and fined a hundred dollars—a fine she refused to pay and the court never collected. Both actions focused attention on the cause.

When the years finally began to take their toll, the two women selected a younger teammate to take over their work. Carrie Chapman Catt, forty years their junior, became executive secretary of the National American Woman Suffrage Association and sent out organizers, raised funds, founded new branches and reinvigorated old ones.

Elizabeth Cady Stanton died in 1902, at the age of eighty-seven. Susan B. Anthony died in 1906, aged eighty-six. For over fifty years the two women had supported and encouraged each other in a monumental civic undertaking.

Mrs. Catt developed the final strategy for adoption of the women's suffrage constitutional amendment. In 1920, sixty-nine years after Susan B. Anthony and Elizabeth Stanton started their crusade in Seneca Falls, the Tennessee legislature approved the women's suffrage amendment to the United States Constitution by a margin of one vote.

When Stanton resigned the presidency of the suffrage movement in 1892, she delivered an eloquent and moving plea to carry on the fight for equal opportunity:

> To guide our own craft, we must be captain, pilot, engineer; with chart and compass to stand at the wheel; to watch the winds and waves, and know when to take in the sail, and to read the signs in the firmament over all. It matters not whether the solitary voyager is man or woman; nature, having endowed them equally, leaves them to their own skill and judgment in the hour of danger, and, if not equal to the occasion, alike they perish.

The voyage through life is often lonely. Companionship makes the trip easier, and usually more enjoyable. In volunteer work, the same principle applies, except that the impact of efforts by two people working in harness often increases logarithmically. Two effective people in tandem are at least four times as effective as one—in some cases, much more than that.

The key to effective teamwork is not the number of people involved, but their ability to work together with single-minded commitment.

Unfortunately, more is not always merrier in volunteer work. Too often, the more people involved in a public-service project, the more effectively they cancel out each other's efforts. Pride and envy too easily undermine most attempts at joint teamwork. As a result, people usually accomplish more working alone than becoming embroiled in hours of debate over objectives and strategies which too often characterize group endeavors.

The object lesson from Addams and Starr; Goodman, Wilson, Krupa and Hampton; Pettit and Stone and De Long; and Stanton and Anthony, is that if you pick the *right* teammate you can accomplish much more than you can ever do alone. But be sure you make the right choice.

> Persons of good sense, I have since observed, seldom fall into disputation, except lawyers, university men, and men of all sorts that have been bred in Edinburgh.
>
> —BENJAMIN FRANKLIN
> (*Autobiography*)

> Give me a man that is capable of a devotion to anything, rather than a cold, calculating average of all the virtues.
>
> —BRET HARTE
> (*The Society upon the Stanislaus*)

> Trust ivrybody—but cut th' ca-ards.
>
> —FINLEY PETER DUNNE
> (*Mr. Dooley's Philosophy*)

Involve Your Family

The measure of a man's success is not the money
he's made. It's the kind of family he's raised.

—JOSEPH P. KENNEDY

In 1811, James Mott was chief clerk in the Philadelphia hardware store operated by a former sea captain,
Thomas Coffin. On April 10, he married the boss's
daughter.

Lucretia Mott had been brought up in Nantucket
where the menfolk were at sea for many months at a
time and community affairs were usually managed by
the women. She had developed a strong sense of
women's rights. Her husband shared her convictions.

Philadelphia was an early home for the movement
to abolish slavery, which was already gathering momentum. Lucretia Mott began to appear on lecture cir-
cuits advocating both women's rights and freedom for
slaves. Her husband accompanied her on these speaking engagements, giving an appearance of substance

and respectability which some of Mrs. Mott's spinster colleagues lacked.

When a leader of the Society of Friends congregation urged parishioners to stop using products of slave labor, Lucretia Mott took the oath never to use cotton cloth, cane sugar or any other slave-produced goods. Although James Mott by now had developed a substantial business in commission sales of cotton, he followed his wife's lead and shifted his business to the less profitable wool trade.

In 1838 Lucretia Mott helped organize the first antislavery convention for American women in Philadelphia. The sessions were held in newly constructed Pennsylvania Hall. Right after the meeting adjourned, a proslavery mob set fire to the building, burning it to the ground. The leaders urged the mob to go to the Mott home on North Ninth Street. James Mott waited patiently with his wife to confront the mob, which fortunately lost interest and never reached its destination.

In 1840, Lucretia Mott was elected a delegate to the World Antislavery Convention in London. When she arrived there she was denied delegate status because of her sex. While in London, she met Elizabeth Cady Stanton, who also had been refused recognition as a delegate because she was female. The two outraged women vowed to take affirmative action to advance the cause of women's rights.

On July 19, 1848, Lucretia Mott and Elizabeth Cady Stanton organized the first American convention on women's rights in Seneca Falls, New York. James Mott was the presiding officer and his wife delivered the opening and closing addresses. Together they had been fighting for the cause for almost forty years.

The torch was passed to Elizabeth Stanton and Susan B. Anthony. Lucretia and James Mott provided support wherever they could, as part of a marriage partnership which lasted fifty-seven years.

Harriot and Sara Hunt, daughters of a shipbuilder, were brought up in Boston early in the nineteenth century. In 1830, Sara became seriously ill, and received all of the accepted medical treatments of the time: leeches, mercury, blisters, prussic acid, calomel. When Sara did not improve, the family consulted a visiting English couple who advocated revolutionary ideas for the treatment of illness: nursing care, rest and proper sanitation practices. Sara recovered rapidly.

The sisters decided to change the medieval practices and superstitions of American medical science. They set to work studying all the available medical literature, rejecting most of it, as they searched for information on disease prevention. Finally, relying on their own common sense, they set up a health-care practice (a license was not required), working with women and children, and emphasizing cleanliness, good diet, bathing, exercise, rest and good nursing care. They achieved cures in case after case where reputable medical doctors had failed using conventional methods.

After Sara was married in 1840, Harriot Hunt continued the practice alone and took an increasingly vocal public role in demanding medical reforms. She advocated health education and gave free public lectures in hygiene. Consultations with women patients persuaded her that there was a need to train women to enter the medical profession. Harriot Hunt sought admission to Harvard Medical School and was twice re-

jected, stirring up a storm which forced medical
schools to open their doors to all qualified students, re-
gardless of sex.

Slowly but surely the Hunt sisters' ideas began to
take hold, and the foundation for modern medical
practice was laid.

Sarah and Angelina Grimké were daughters of the
chief justice of South Carolina. One of their brothers
was a judge of the Supreme Court of Ohio and another
was a member of the South Carolina State Senate.

During their upbringing, the Grimké sisters witnessed harsh and unfair treatment of slaves in their
own household. Sarah was particularly outraged by
the prohibition against teaching slaves how to read.
She surreptitiously gave lessons to her own maid and
was threatened with severe punishment.

In 1821, Sarah Grimké visited Philadelphia,
where she first encountered the Quakers and their
strenuous stand against slavery. She joined the Society of Friends and decided to stay in Philadelphia.
Her younger sister, Angelina, joined her. Both girls
were soon caught up in the antislavery movement organized by Lucretia Mott. Angelina wrote an antislavery
pamphlet entitled *An Appeal to the Christian Women
of the South,* which was published in 1836. The pamphlet urged women to persuade their husbands to end
the institution of slavery. Postmasters in South Carolina destroyed copies of the pamphlet before they
reached their addresses. Angelina Grimké was warned
that she would be placed under arrest if she ever returned to her home state.

Sarah Grimké followed with her own pamphlet,
entitled *Epistle to the Clergy of the Southern States,*

criticizing the attempt to use the Bible to justify the institution of slavery. The firsthand source of both writings gave them credibility and increased their impact.

The sisters were recruited by the American Antislavery Society to go on a lecture tour of New York and New England before women's meetings. In Lynn, Massachusetts, they appeared before a mixed audience of men and women, contrary to the accepted mores of the day. The Congregational clergy of New England issued a "Pastoral Letter" objecting to their unwomanly behavior and the Grimké sisters picked up the gauntlet. Sarah responded to the "Pastoral Letter" in the Boston *Spectator,* likening the Congregational elders to the judges at the Salem witch trials who "solemnly condemned nineteen persons and one dog to death for witchcraft." The clergy responded by prohibiting parishioners from attending meetings at which the Grimkés were scheduled to speak.

By the time the Grimkés reached Boston, the audiences at their lectures numbered in the thousands. Their courage and spunk proved to be just the tonic New England needed, and the antislavery movement gained momentum and supporters quickly.

"Like father, like son" is an aphorism based on experience, so it is not surprising to find many outstanding men and women whose values were developed from parental examples and teachings. Affirmative action, however, requires something more in the form of family interaction, and that is the basis for the example presented below.

Before turning to that example, there is one other that deserves mention—that of militant abolitionist

John Brown and his five sons, who not only followed their father as advocates of a cause but two of whom willingly gave up their lives in the process. History has not treated John Brown kindly. He has been generally dismissed as a wild-eyed zealot. But by his own values he was a martyr to the ideal of freedom. He foresaw, much as Thomas Paine had done almost a century before, that the only resolution to the slavery issue would come from violent confrontation; and after a quarter of a century of unproductive debate over abolition, he was willing to be the firebrand to bring the issue to its final violent stages in Kansas and at Harpers Ferry. He had the full support and devotion of his family in the cause. Two of his sons died in the futile assault on the federal munitions depot, but they believed in what he was trying to do. Brown's eloquent self-defense during his trial for treason is one of the great statements of human ideals in the country's history.

Historians Henry Pringle and Richard Hofstadter portrayed Theodore Roosevelt as something of an ambitious buffoon. What they failed to perceive was the unique political phenomenon TR represented—an officeholder who was a free man, motivated by his own perceptions of what was right and wrong.

TR reached the White House through his own personal efforts, which gave him the luxury of genuine *independence* to do as he pleased in office. He had an unparalleled opportunity to carry out idealistic principles rather than currying favor with political leaders and big contributors.

When Theodore Roosevelt declared his belief in

the common man, he *meant* it. It was not political oratory prepared by a political consultant after analyzing the latest polls. He wanted to do the *right* thing, not for his place in history, but because that was the way his parents had raised him, and that was the direction his sister Bannie continued to push him.

He was actually Theodore Roosevelt, *Junior,* and his father, now forgotten to history, was a man of accomplishment, independence and high purpose. Father Roosevelt lavished attention on his children as they grew up, especially on his oldest child, Anna (Bannie), who suffered from Pott's disease—tuberculosis of the spine—when she was very young. This resulted in a lifelong disability, leaving her housebound. But she was a major source of support and guidance for her younger brother, Theodore Junior, in his public career.

The older Theodore Roosevelt enjoyed the economic freedom produced by the family's successful plate glass and mirror business, which had been founded by his father and was now managed by his brothers. He gave much of his time to humanitarian causes and good works, and was widely applauded for his civic leadership. He was one of the original founders of the Metropolitan Museum of Art, the American Museum of Natural History, the Children's Aid Society, the New York Orthopedic Dispensary and Hospital, and the Newsboys' Lodging House, and was constantly raising money for such causes. He also helped raise funds for the base of the Statue of Liberty, and aided the movement to transport Cleopatra's Needle to Central Park.

TR Senior was no checkbook philanthropist. He

worked at his causes personally. During the Depression of 1873, he visited hospital wards, prisons and slums. He lobbied for improvements in the city's insane asylums on Ward's and Blackwell's islands.

Balancing off the happy times spent with an attentive father were the personal tragedies that touched the Roosevelt household. In addition to Bannie's illness was young Theodore's asthma, which kept him frail and sickly.

His father died at the age of forty-six while TR Junior was a sophomore at college. The loss of his idol pained the young man deeply.

A few years later tragedy struck again—this time a double one—his young wife died in childbirth from Bright's disease, and his mother died of typhoid fever, both within hours of each other. There was a double funeral.

Theodore Roosevelt, Jr., was twenty-five years old at the time, and now his only source of family support was his older sister, Bannie. She continued to perform that role for the rest of his life, even after Theodore remarried and was raising his own family, and after she married and became a mother.

Reform politics was the dominant interest for Theodore Roosevelt, Sr., during his son's adolescence. It was among the younger man's lasting memories of the man he adored and hoped to emulate. His father's brother, Robert, a prominent Democrat, had set a standard of political probity when he became an active leader of the Committee of Seventy, organized to rid New York City of the Tweed Ring. Uncle Robert had publicly denounced Boss Tweed and Tammany Hall politics in a speech in the Great Hall at Cooper Union, and after Tweed's fall, he was widely admired for his reform leadership.

On the Republican side, Theodore Roosevelt Senior had demanded reform in his party when the second Grant administration began producing one major national scandal after another. The leading political power in Washington was Senator Roscoe Conkling of Utica, New York, a master at machine politics and grand master of Republican patronage. Theodore Roosevelt Senior helped block Conkling's nomination for President at the Republican national convention of 1876. He later allowed himself to be nominated by Rutherford B. Hayes to become collector of customs in New York, replacing Conkling's hand-picked appointee, Chester A. Arthur.

Conkling took considerable pleasure in blocking Roosevelt's nomination in the Senate as a matter of personal privilege. When Roosevelt learned that his nomination had been killed, he was already on his deathbed. He wrote to his son at Harvard what is believed to have been his last letter reporting the Senate's action, claiming to be relieved at the outcome:

> I feel sorry for the country, however, as it shows the power of partisan politicians who think of nothing higher than their own interests. I fear for your future. We cannot stand so corrupt a government for any great length of time.

The words sank in. After his father's death a few weeks later, TR declared that he would keep his father's letters, including the last one, as "talismans against evil."

The memory of his father and what he stood for remained with the son throughout his public career. After the McKinley assassination, TR's first day in the White House coincided with his father's birthday. That evening Roosevelt told his sisters and their husbands, "I feel as if my father's hand were on my shoulder."

During his presidency, Bannie lived in a house on N Street, which came to be known as "the little White House" because of the President's regular visits and consultations.

Except for an assassin's bullet, resulting in President McKinley's death, TR probably would have gone on to quiet obscurity instead of becoming one of the most freewheeling, unbossed Presidents in the nation's history. "That damned cowboy" is what the head of the Republican party regulars, Mark Hanna, called him, and with good reason.

Unimpeded by political debts, and with his father's reforming zeal to guide him, President Theodore Roosevelt set the country on its ear by:

—launching the most daring conservation policy in the nation's history, in defiance of coal, oil and lumbering interests;

—initiating the first antitrust prosecutions in the nation's history, against the top financial and railroad interests in the country;

—engineering a revolution in Panama to facilitate the building of the "Great Ditch," one of the boldest engineering feats of its time;

—personally interceding in the settlement of a major national strike and confronting powerful mineowners nose-to-nose;

—haranguing "malefactors of great wealth" who ordinarily were the principal sources of Republican party campaign contributions.

These were not the achievements of one man. They were the cumulative results of family values and direction.

His father would indeed have been proud of him. His sister certainly was.

Few things are more heartwarming than watching a family act together as a unit. Whether going off on a picnic, cleaning the garage, or heading for church, the family unit represents the strongest bond of humankind. Sadly, many families never experience the joy of the tight family relationship, but those who do are thrice blessed.

The family is particularly effective in performing public-service projects. Every community, every school, every congregation benefits from the generous acts of parents and their children supporting each other and working together on projects ranging from baking cookies at home for church fairs to selling boxes of store-bought ones for the Girl Scouts. Such family activities are so commonplace we take them for granted—they are the social cement which separates civilized communities from barbarian invaders. What is more unusual is to find families working together in sustained public-service activities after the offspring have reached adulthood, at the time when most children have set off on their own careers or have started their own families.

There are notable examples in the creative arts and science. In the field of English literature the

Brontë sisters supported each other as children and adults. Théo Van Gogh played an essential part in making possible his brother Vincent's brief but brilliant period of intense creative work. The joint research of Marie and Pierre Curie led to practical use of radiation therapy. In history there are the husband-and-wife teams Will and Ariel Durant (history of philosophy) and Charles and Mary Beard. In anthropology there is the Leakey family's research into the beginnings of man in Africa. In modern industrial management, there is the pioneering work of Frank and Lillian Gilbreth in production and personnel techniques—while parenting twelve offspring (two of whom authored the delightful family revelations in *Cheaper by the Dozen*).

The real test of family strength comes in the tough, long battles for causes. Here is where family mettle is tested over the long haul.

The "family" has become unfashionable during our period of concern over equal rights for the individual. Yet anyone who has experienced the warmth and strength of the close-knit family unit knows that it is the backbone of all civilization.

When members of a family can share in a public-service project, not only does the project benefit, but the family does, too. Family bonds are strengthened by a joint experience which gives a sense of accomplishment to every single one of the participants.

Going Into
Action

Get the Facts

Everybody's business is nobody's business.
Nobody's business is my business.

—CLARA BARTON

In 1772, Thomas Paine traveled from Lewes to London to present the grievances of his fellow British customs officers to representatives of the government and members of Parliament. He had written his case out carefully beforehand: how the low wages of those responsible for detecting smuggling and for imposing duties had caused so much hardship that the men were forced to take bribes in order to provide for their families. Increasing their pay would increase the amount of duties collected by the Crown, and also halt the spread of corruption.

The reaction of government officials should have been predictable: Instead of raising wages for the excise men, they discharged Thomas Paine for neglect of duty.

He had been supplementing his income after hours by running a grocery and tobacco shop owned by his mother-in-law. His trip to London had caused the

shop to be shut down. It soon was forced into bank-
ruptcy. Paine's outraged wife abandoned him. To
avoid debtors' prison, he sold all his furniture and possessions. At the age of forty-six, Paine found himself
unemployed and penniless.

Thomas Paine had one resource left—a letter of
introduction written for him by Benjamin Franklin
when the latter had seen some of his writing during
a visit to London as commissioner for the Colonies.
Franklin's letter was addressed to his son-in-law in
Philadelphia and asked him to help Paine find
work.

Thomas Paine arrived in Philadelphia exactly
four months before the bloodshed at Lexington and
Concord. He witnessed firsthand the doubts and un-
certainties that were tearing the Colonies apart. In response to the British military buildup and the bloody
confrontations in Massachusetts, most colonists fa-
vored a course of appeasement and compromise.
Franklin, Washington and Jefferson were urging responsible citizens to maintain their loyalty to the
Crown of England and seek only to have abuses corrected. The Continental Congress, meeting in Philadelphia where Paine was living, twice reaffirmed its
allegiance to Great Britain.

Thomas Paine held a different view. His own experience with British officials, combined with years of
watching his family struggle against poverty in
England while a small landed aristocracy enjoyed
wealth and power, convinced him that the only course
for America was total independence. He spent the fall
of 1775 setting his arguments down on paper, present-
ing the case for immediate separation from the mother

country. He supported his conclusions with detailed facts.

Paine wrote that the decision was critical to the future of mankind:

> 'Tis not the concern of a day, a year or an age; posterity is involved in the contest.

At the suggestion of Benjamin Rush, Paine entitled his pamphlet *Common Sense.* He took the manuscript to a printer in Philadelphia, and paid him out of his own pocket to print a thousand copies.

The edition sold out in a week. Paine reinvested the proceeds into additional printings. Within three months he had sold over a hundred thousand copies. The price was so low that Paine never realized any profit from the sales, but he watched his ideas ignite a fire that raced through the Colonies.

George Washington hailed Paine's pamphlet as "sound doctrine and unanswerable reasoning." John Adams said that it would make the independence movement a matter of "common faith"; his wife, Abigail, described it as a "ray of revelation."

Less than six months after the first appearance of *Common Sense,* the Colonies united to adopt a Declaration of Independence. Virtually all Paine's principles were included in the document.

Historians hail *Common Sense* as a great example of effective pamphleteering, and it is credited as a major factor in shaping the destiny of the United States.

Two significant factors are important to those who want to render similar public service:

(1) Thomas Paine's own vision and perseverance

produced the text for *Common Sense*. No one hired him
or forced him to do it. He saw the need and went to
work assembling his own facts and arguments. Self-reliance produced the final product.

(2) Paine himself arranged for the pamphlet's
publication. He did not depend on any trade publisher,
motivated by profit, to decide whether the pamphlet
should appear, or when, or how.

Self-publishing has long been honorable in literary cir-
cles. It has provided public access to the early works of
many of the world's great poets—Shelley, Byron, Poe,
Whitman, Sandburg; all of whom themselves published their own first books of poems. Many of
America's outstanding authors also self-published
their first works—Henry David Thoreau, Stephen
Crane, Zane Grey. People are always surprised to discover that one of America's basic cookbooks, *The Joy of
Cooking*, with sales now in the millions, was originally
self-published by its determined creator.

The explanation is simple: The number one yard-
stick of commercial book publishers for accepting a
manuscript is its market potential—how many copies
will it sell? Literary merit, substantive ideas, public
benefit are almost always subsidiary to the main question: Will it make money?*

Most good causes—like Paine's plea for independence—are not profit-oriented.

If yours is a text arguing a cause that depends on
educating the public, self-publish. Do not become discouraged by rejection slips from trade publishers.

---

* Publishers protest that there are some books they publish for literary
reasons rather than profit, but these are pitifully few.

Dealing with such publishers will usually bring defeat before the start of the battle.

Many people have the impression that commercial book publishers control access to the printing presses, and that if a commercial house does not accept your book, it cannot be printed. This is far from the truth. Only one major book publishing company—Doubleday—operates its own printing plant. Most books are manufactured by independent presses whose sole business is printing books for many different publishers. These presses compete for the work by submitting estimates for each job. Some printers are large, some are small. Most university-press books are published by short-run companies, which will typeset, print and bind as few as a hundred or two hundred copies of a book. The industry handbook, *Literary Market Place,* which is available in most public libraries, lists these and other publishing services. There are also many helpful handbooks on self-publishing.*

Self-publishing is entirely different from "vanity publishing." Self-publishing means that *you* oversee the book manufacture, distribution and sales. (The handbooks tell you how.) Vanity publishing, on the other hand, involves hiring a specialty firm to do the job for you, *pretending* that the book is being issued by a trade publisher, when in fact the vanity publisher is making its profit from the *author* rather than from sales of the book. Most vanity-press books look the part—poor design, pulpy paper, cheap covers.

---

* The most useful of these, in the author's judgment, is Dan Poynter's *The Self-Publishing Manual,* self-published by Parachuting Publications, P.O. Box 4232, Santa Barbara, California 93103 ($9.95 postpaid).

Self-published books, even if amateurish, usually reflect the author's commitment. Vanity-press books show the manufacturer's disdain and boredom.

Self-published books reflect the author's heart and mind. Vanity-press books usually only reflect the author's ego. If you want to publish, do it yourself.

Books—whether self-published or trade-published—can be powerful weapons for good. Some are written to expose harsh facts (like Michael Harrington's *The Other America*), to fictionalize emotion-charged conditions (like Harriet Beecher Stowe's *Uncle Tom's Cabin*), or to advocate national policy changes (like Ralph Nader's *Unsafe At Any Speed* or Jonathan Schell's book on nuclear war, *The Fall of the Earth*). A book by itself can accomplish remarkable things.

Here are some important examples of what only a tiny handful of individuals have been able to achieve through the writing and publication of books:

Helen Hunt Jackson's *A Century of Dishonor*, published in 1881, brought about a basic change in United States policy toward the American Indian, and the first recognition of Indian rights. Mrs. Jackson was a poet who had moved to Colorado Springs for her health in 1873. There she learned about the plight of the Indians, who were being victimized by inept and often corrupt agents sent from Washington. After months of careful research, she documented charges of mismanagement and injustice by the federal government, which generated public pressure on Congress and the President for reform.

Jacob Riis created the impetus for housing reform in 1890 with his book *How the Other Half Lives*. Riis had worked for ten years as a police reporter in New York City, and had seen firsthand the festering slum conditions of the Lower East Side. Shortly after the book appeared, Riis met young Theodore Roosevelt, the new chairman of the police commission in New York, whose office was just across the street. The two men made joint visits to inspect tenement conditions and inept police performance in the city's slum districts. Throughout his later career, Roosevelt repeatedly pressed for improvement in living conditions for the poor, while Riis continued to turn out articles and books. The result in time was not only stricter housing codes, but the eventual launching of the nation's massive low-income-housing construction program.

In 1903 appeared *The Woman Who Toils,* a book written jointly by sisters-in-law, Marie and Bessie Van Vorst. The book had a major impact on the movement to improve factory working conditions for women and children.

After Bessie's husband died, the two women moved to France, where they collaborated on a novel. Then they returned to the United States and went to work under assumed names in factories in different parts of the country. Marie Van Vorst worked in a shoe factory in Lynn, Massachusetts, and then in several cotton mills in the South; her sister-in-law worked in a pickle factory in Pittsburgh, then in a Buffalo knitting mill. They wrote graphic descriptions based on their firsthand experiences of the harsh conditions under which women and young girls were forced to work, and helped to generate the public demands for reform that led finally to wage and hour legislation.

Ida Tarbell spent two years studying all aspects of

the oil industry before publishing her landmark *History of the Standard Oil Company* in 1904, exposing the system of secret railroad rebates used by John D. Rockefeller and his associates. The book opened the eyes of the American public to business abuses, and set the stage for the first enforcement of the Sherman Antitrust Act during the Theodore Roosevelt administration.

The best-selling American book in 1906 was a self-published novel by a reformer who exposed the harsh and unsanitary working conditions in the Chicago stockyards. Upton Sinclair's *The Jungle* described the corruption of government meat inspectors who approved sick and dying cattle and hogs, the rat carcasses that found their way into ground meat used to make sausages, and the filthy environment in which much of the country's meat was prepared for human consumption. When President Theodore Roosevelt read the book he immediately launched a campaign for stricter meat inspection legislation and a new Pure Food Act. Five trade book publishers rejected the book before Sinclair decided to self-publish it.

Rachel Carson's *Silent Spring*, which appeared in 1962, was probably the single most important force in the development of environmental awareness in the United States. Ms. Carson's documentation of the impact of agricultural chemicals, especially DDT, on the environment not only triggered strong legislative measures to curb the use of toxic chemicals, but helped generate momentum behind the entire national environmental protection movement itself. While Ms. Carson was a staff biologist and an editor for the U.S. Bureau of Fisheries, and later for the U.S. Fish and

Wildlife Service, she spent her spare time after hours
and on weekends producing three works about the life
of the sea (*Under the Sea Wind, The Sea Around Us,*
and *The Edge of the Sea*). Then one day a friend in
Massachusetts asked her to help stop the use of DDT in
local mosquito-control programs because it was killing
birds as well as insects. Ms. Carson realized that only a
massive public-education effort could produce any significant change. She turned to the writing of *Silent
Spring* with a reformer's zeal. After the book appeared,
the chemical industry spent huge sums on public-rela-
tions initiatives in an effort to overcome the book's impact, but these efforts only served to strengthen the
book's message.

Although suffering from bone cancer and crip-
pling arthritis during the final months of writing, Ms.
Carson was determined to finish the job. She knew she
was not writing for herself, but for those who would
carry on the fight. The book's acknowledgments revealed the character and motivation of the author:

> I must acknowledge our vast indebtedness to a
> host of people, many of them unknown to me person-
> ally, who have nevertheless made the writing of this
> book seem worthwhile. These are the poeple who first
> spoke out against the reckless and irresponsible poi-
> soning of the world that man shares with all other
> creatures, and who are even now fighting the thou-
> sands of small battles that in the end will bring victory
> for sanity and common sense. . . .

Books are not the only weapons in the battle of facts
against injury and injustice.

High on the list of American reformers is
Dorothea Lynde Dix. Daughter of an itinerant Meth-

odist minister and a semi-invalid mother, she was raised by her grandmother and great-aunt in Massachusetts. At the age of fourteen, Dorothea Dix opened a school for small children; at sixteen, a school for young girls. By the time she was twenty-two, Ms. Dix had published an elementary science textbook. She was bothered by periodic spells of illness and seemed a perfect prototype of the nineteenth-century New England spinster. Then one day in March 1841, when she was thirty-nine, a Harvard Divinity School student asked her to teach a Sunday-school class at the East Cambridge jail. When she visited the jail, she discovered that the inmates included not only vagrants and petty criminals, but also a group of women whose sole offense was insanity. They occupied foul, cold quarters. When Ms. Dix complained to the jailer, he responded that lunatics do not feel the cold.

A few days later, Dorothea Dix appeared in the town court to complain to the judge about the treatment of the mentally ill inmates, and set off a storm of shocked reaction in the local press. One reader came forward with funds to provide heat and renovation of the quarters in which the women were housed.

But Dorothea Dix knew that repairs and heat were not the solution to the community's ignorant, heartless approach to the problem of mental illness. Her life's work now became clear. She had to do something to change public attitudes and community treatment for the mentally disabled.

The first step was to collect the facts.

She read everything she could lay her hands on, and learned that intelligent, sympathetic care for the insane could actually produce positive results.

Then she set out to survey every jail and house of correction in the Commonwealth of Massachusetts. She spent eighteen months at the task, filling her notebook with descriptions of persons confined in "cages, closets, cellars, stalls, pens." She saw them naked, chained, frequenty beaten and lashed into obedience.

In January 1843 Dorothea Dix submitted a detailed memorandum to the Massachusetts legislature describing her findings. After weeks of debate, the legislature appropriated funds to expand an experimental mental-illness treatment program established at Worcester a few years before at the urging of Horace Mann.

Dorothea Dix next launched investigations of conditions in Rhode Island and New York. In both states she succeeded in persuading the legislatures to provide funds for decent care facilities. Then she went to New Jersey, where she persuaded the legislature to establish the state's first mental hospital.

Over the next three years, Ms. Dix traveled thirty thousand miles, inspecting the pitiful conditions under which the mentally ill were confined in Pennsylvania, Kentucky, Maryland, Ohio, Illinois, Mississippi, Alabama, Tennessee and North Carolina. Support for her work grew, and state after state changed its policies toward the mentally ill.

When fatigue and illness finally forced her to slow down, Dorothea Dix went to Europe for a rest. Soon she was back on her feet crusading for her cause. At her urging, the British government established a commission to inquire into the treatment of the mentally ill in Scotland. She even called on Pope Pius IX and

extracted his personal assurance that conditions in
Italy would be investigated and corrected.

The New England schoolmarm and her arsenal of
hard facts had helped to improve the world.

Clara Barton was working in the U.S. Patent Office in
Washington when the Civil War broke out. When she
discovered that there was a shortage of first-aid supplies at the Battle of Bull Run, she advertised in her
hometown newspaper in Massachusetts for gifts of
bandages, medicine and food. Barton collected the
shipments and distributed them by mule team to military hospitals and on battlefields. Her activities increased in response to heavy casualties in battles
nearer Washington. Avoiding the delays and red tape
of both the U.S. Sanitary Commission and the Army
Nurse Corps, Clara Barton provided direct volunteer
service at a series of military engagements, often com-
mandeering army mules and wagons to transport her
emergency medical provisions. Thousands of wounded
soldiers referred to her as the "Angel of the Battlefield."

Not satisfied with rendering direct care and aid
herself, Ms. Barton started asking hard questions
about the poor quality of the medical services provided
to the wounded at the front. She presented facts show-
ing the inadequacies of the Surgeon-General's division
to a congressional committee. The press publicized her
efforts, which in turn produced more contributions of
supplies.

At war's end, Clara Barton set up an office to obtain information about missing soldiers for distraught
families.

In late 1868, exhausted by increasing demands on her as a lecturer, Clara Barton traveled to Europe for some rest. In Switzerland she learned about a group organized by a Swiss banker troubled by the lack of medical care on the battlefield of Solferino in 1859. The group was called the International Committee of the Red Cross. Eleven governments had ratified a treaty which provided neutrality for volunteers working under the emblem of a red cross on a white background (the reverse of the Swiss flag). Clara Barton learned that the United States had not ratified the treaty because of opposition from the State Department.

Clara Barton was soon back in the United States organizing an American Red Cross Committee and seeking Senate approval of the Geneva Convention. Hard as it may be to believe today, approval of the Red Cross treaty was a long and difficult struggle.

In the face of arguments that the Monroe Doctrine prohibited any involvement in international agreements, Barton became a one-person crusade, hammering away at the State Department, the White House and Congress. She gathered facts, published and distributed pamphlets, wrote newspaper articles and gave public lectures. Every time there was a natural disaster, she used the facts to point out the absence of organized relief efforts of the type the Red Cross could provide.

On March 1, 1882, after more than ten years of untiring campaigning by Ms. Barton, President Chester A. Arthur signed the Geneva Treaty with the full approval of the Secretary of State and the United States Senate.

Clara Barton became the first chairman of the

American Red Cross. She functioned as its chief executive for over twenty years, directing relief activities, providing emergency aid for areas struck by hurricanes, yellow fever, floods and other cataclysms. She expanded Red Cross services to provide not only emergency relief but also rehabilitation assistance. When floods struck the Ohio and Mississippi valleys, Red Cross boats carried emergency relief supplies and materials for rebuilding houses and barns. When a hurricane devastated the Galveston, Texas, area in 1900, Clara Barton arranged for the Red Cross to supply 1,500,000 strawberry plants to help the farmers get reestablished.

Clara Barton learned, through a lifetime of using facts to get results, that there was a too-long-overlooked fact about public service—there is little gratitude, and much resistance that must be overcome:

> The paths of charity are over roadways of ashes; and he who would tread them must be prepared to meet opposition, misconstruction, jealousy and calumny. Let his work be that of angels, still it will not satisfy all.

Florence Kelley was an effective reform pamphleteer in early twentieth-century America. She assembled facts about the exploitation of women and children in factories, and wrote pamphlets and books to influence legislation that would limit working hours and child labor. Her most serious setback came in 1905, when the United States Supreme Court declared unconstitutional a New York State statute limiting factory labor by women to ten hours a day. The decision in *Lochner* v. *New York* contained language suggesting that reconsideration of the issue might be possible if justification could be shown for utilizing the state's police power to override "the obligations of private contract."

Ms. Kelley was head of the National Consumers' League, which used consumer pressure to force proper working conditions on manufacturers. She started looking for the opportunity to overturn the *Lochner* ruling, which jeopardized all the reform work she and her colleagues had been doing. The chance came three years later when the Supreme Court agreed to hear a case challenging the constitutionality of an Oregon statute setting a maximum of ten hours of labor a day for women.

Kelley decided to try to enlist the aid of Louis D. Brandeis, a successful Boston corporation lawyer who had shown a sympathetic interest in public issues through a series of cases he had brought against utilities and insurance companies. Accompanied by Josephine Goldmark, a cousin of Brandeis's wife, Florence Kelley called on Brandeis, who agreed to take on the difficult Supreme Court defense of the Oregon law, provided she would assemble sociological and medical data demonstrating that longer working hours for women had an adverse effect on their health and welfare.

The brief which Brandeis submitted to the United States Supreme Court consisted of only *two* pages of legal citations to precedents and authorities, and *more than a hundred* pages of employment statistics and studies. It was a revolutionary approach to a legal argument (and was to become legendary in law schools as the "Brandeis brief"). Louis Brandeis's factual arguments carried the day, and the statutory limitation on working hours for women at last was upheld as a constitutional exercise of police power for the public welfare.

Primary reliance on facts was the hallmark of Brandeis's professional career. Time and again he spent days learning the factual background of legal problems so that he understood the feasibility of various solutions that might be suggested, making it possible for him to concentrate on results and not just legalistic concepts.

In 1912, Brandeis sent a congratulatory letter to Woodrow Wilson following his nomination as Democratic party candidate for President. Brandeis was invited to have lunch with the candidate at his retreat in Sea Girt, New Jersey. The luncheon lasted more than three hours. Brandeis and Wilson discussed a wide range of major issues confronting the nation. The candidate took an immediate liking to Brandeis and formed a deep trust in his experience and judgment. Because Wilson was not familiar with the world of business, at his request Brandeis prepared a detailed campaign statement of economic policies to promote competition and control big business.

After Wilson was elected President, he considered adding Brandeis to his cabinet, but encountered so much opposition from business and financial leaders that he concluded it would be wiser to consult the lawyer as an informal adviser instead. In that capacity, Brandeis played a major role in drafting the legislation to create the Federal Trade Commission, and in the preparation of the Clayton Act, authorizing private suits to enforce the antitrust laws.

When Wilson nominated Brandeis to be an associate justice of the United States Supreme Court, Senate confirmation hearings dragged on for over four months. Leaders of the business and financial establishment attacked Brandeis for his antibusiness record. President A. Lawrence Lowell of Harvard University was one of fifty-five prominent citizens of Boston who signed a petition opposing confirmation. Just beneath the surface of the attacks against Brandeis for his "radical" economic theories, of course, was the fact that Brandeis would be the first person of Jewish background to serve on the Supreme Court. Bigotry was his leading opponent, rather than any argument on the merits of his appointment. Finally, the Senate, voting along strict party lines, confirmed President Wilson's nomination, and Louis D. Brandeis began his twenty-year service as an associate justice of the United States Supreme Court—a service that would be marked by distinction as he marshaled factual arguments to support progressive legislation to improve social and economic conditions.

On the day he was confirmed by the Senate, Brandeis received a succinct communication from one of his new colleagues, a one-word telegram reading: WELCOME. It was signed by Oliver Wendell Holmes. In later years, Holmes and Brandeis were teamed in powerful dissents again and again in opposition to the Supreme Court's deeply conservative majority.

Louis Brandeis believed that lawyers had a special public responsibility in a modern industrial society. Speaking before the Harvard Ethical Society in 1905, prior to joining the Supreme Court, Brandeis spoke out against "leading lawyers" who used their skills primarily in the defense of business interests:

Instead of holding a position of independence, between the wealthy and the people, prepared to curb the excesses of either, able lawyers have, to a large extent, allowed themselves to become adjuncts of great corporations and have neglected the obligation to use their powers for the protection of the people.

Brandeis himself spent part of every day working for the public interest. His long-range goal was to be free to concentrate entirely on *pro bono* matters.

The atmosphere at his law office had been all work and no play. During the winter, the temperature was set so low that visitors usually wore their overcoats and did not waste time in chitchat. Brandeis kept his nose to the grindstone and continued to earn big fees, which he put into conservative investments in order to acquire the independence that was to come in his later years.

He explained his parsimonious approach in these words:

I have only one life, and it is short enough. Why waste it on things I don't want most? I don't want money or property most. I want to be free.

By learning how to find the truth, Brandeis was able to achieve freedom as a lawyer, as a reformer, and as a judicial officer in the highest court in the land.

Truth is a mighty sword. Too many worthy causes have been lost because they were founded on emotion instead of facts. If a cause is worth fighting for, it is worth taking the time to dig out the facts that support it as well as those that will destroy the opposition.

Access to facts is surprisingly easy. The place to

begin is usually with the reference librarian at a good public library.* Professional librarians are committed to helping patrons find the information they want without prying into the reason or being defensive and protective.

Never settle for secondary sources if primary ones are available. Go see for yourself. Talk directly to the people involved. Never assume anything. Take photographs. Make your own notes. Build a clipping file. Never assume anything. Become an expert. Get the facts, but be sure they are right. *Never assume anything.*

* Preserving and enhancing the country's public-library resources is itself a cause worthy of any concerned American, for in those resources are the tools for future Paines, Carsons, Bartons and Brandeises to protect our independence, our values, our heritage.

CHAPTER 11

Pick a Good Fight

It's not the size of the dog in the fight,
it's the size of the fight in the dog.

—KIT RAYMOND, crew coach

Henry L. Stimson was an accomplished New York trial lawyer with a strong sense of ethics, an excellent organizing ability and a commitment to the country's welfare. He served as United States Attorney for the Southern District of New York under President Theodore Roosevelt. He served as Secretary of War under President William Howard Taft; was sent on a special mission to Central America in 1927 by President Calvin Coolidge; was appointed Secretary of State by President Herbert Hoover in 1929; and again served as Secretary of War under President Franklin D. Roosevelt from 1940 through World War II.

Stimson personified the high-minded private citizen, always on call to serve his nation. He believed that public business should be conducted in a fashion that would inspire confidence, with no hint of personal ambition or official misconduct.

Stimson had a capacity for righteous indignation when he saw something that was wrong and needed correcting. He always seemed ready to fight against injustice and incompetence. As a private lawyer he delighted in writing letters to public agencies and big corporations, calling them on the carpet for improper acts or thoughtless conduct.

Riding the subway one day, Stimson witnessed an impatient conductor close the car door on the knuckles of a small boy, causing pain and injury. As soon as he reached his office, Stimson wrote a detailed report about the incident which he sent off to the president of the Inter-Borough Rapid Transit company, demanding immediate action.

If the Long Island Rail Road was inexcusably behind schedule, or if trains were unclean or overcrowded, Stimson would send off missives to top railroad officials telling them exactly what was wrong.

He warned the recipients of his letters that he intended to continue to cause them trouble until they concluded it would be easier to correct the problem than put up with his nagging. He meant it, too, and he usually got results.

What is remarkable about Henry Stimson's example is that he was never too busy or too involved in weighty world affairs to make the effort to fight against little wrongs which affected everyday people.

Sometimes "doing battle" involves only a single act.

One day the driver of the bus in which Mrs. Rosa Parks was riding in Montgomery, Alabama, called out

to her, "Niggers move back." It was Thursday evening,
December 1, 1955, and Mrs. Parks, weighted down with
a load of groceries, was bone-weary after a long day's
work. The bus had been empty when she got aboard,
and she had taken a seat in the first row of the section
marked "Whites Only." Before long the bus filled up.
When two white male passengers got on board, the
driver attempted to evict Mrs. Parks to make seats
available for the men.

She acted as if she had not heard the driver's of-
fensive command. The driver pulled the bus to a stop,
got out of his seat and confronted his obstinate passen-
ger directly, repeating his command.

Mrs. Parks would not budge.

The driver called the police, and she was placed
under arrest.

When she was permitted to do so, Mrs. Parks tele-
phoned E. V. Nixon, an officer of the local branch of
the National Association for the Advancement of Colored People, and asked him if he could help her raise
bail. Nixon immediately consulted a Birmingham lawyer, and together the two men mapped out a plan not
only to provide bail and legal defense for Mrs. Parks,
but also to seize the chance to attack the constitutionality of the segregation statute under which she had been
arrested. Both men were aware that such a battle
might be long and costly, but they also knew that a
victory could be a major blow to the South's "Jim
Crow" laws.

Nixon called on the new pastor of the Dexter Ave-
nue Church, Dr. Martin Luther King, Jr., and asked
the young minister if he would help build community
support for Mrs. Parks's cause.

Dr. King presided over a meeting of community leaders in his church the following afternoon. They decided to ask the entire black community to boycott all Montgomery buses the following Monday. Many of those who attended the meeting doubted that the black residents—disheartened and disorganized as a result of past defeats—would respond to the call for a boycott, particularly since the weather was raw and most of the people had long distances to travel to their places of employment.

Handbills, newspaper stories, telephone calls and word-of-mouth contact over the weekend produced an almost 100 percent boycott of Montgomery buses on Monday morning. Black taxicab drivers helped out by agreeing to carry older passengers to work for the same charge as standard bus fares.

Meanwhile, in the Montgomery city courtroom, Mrs. Parks's attorney moved to dismiss the charges against her on the ground that enforced segregation of public transportation violated the United States Constitution. The judge denied the motion and found Mrs. Parks guilty. He imposed a fine of ten dollars and costs.

That evening at seven o'clock, a mass meeting was held by the boycott organizers to discuss the events of the day and to plan the future course of conduct.

Dr. King took the rostrum as coordinator of the anti-discrimination drive. He urged his listeners above all not to give in to bitterness, but instead to fight with quiet courage. His plea became the rallying cry for the ultimately successful constitutional battle that followed, marking a major turning point in the civil rights history of the United States:

Future historians will say, "There lived a great people—a black people—who injected new meaning and dignity into the veins of civilization."

The old French Quarter in New Orleans owes its preservation largely to the efforts of a single person, Elizabeth Thomas Werlein. Mrs. Werlein moved into the French Quarter in the early twentieth century and became entranced with its architectural traditions and history. She published a booklet of photographs of the wrought-iron railings, only to learn that many of the railings had been removed even before her book was off the presses. She began urging area residents to restore many of the old mansions and preserve their unique ironwork balconies.

When Prohibition brought brothels, nightclubs and speakeasies into the Vieux Carré, jeopardizing the historic character of the area, Mrs. Werlein got tough. She organized a property owners' association, spearheaded the enactment of zoning regulations and strict building codes, and instituted court actions to block the mindless destruction of buildings. She fought every effort by commercial interests to destroy the character of the French Quarter, and soon won the cooperation of city and state officials. As a result of her single-minded work over the years, the historic center of old New Orleans is now officially registered as one of the country's finest architectural landmarks.

When the land occupied by the Paiute Indians in the Far West was overrun by white settlers, the Indians fought back. Then the Paiutes were confined to a small reservation, where conditions were intolerable, and which was under the supervision of inept Indian agents sent out from Washington. When starvation forced the Paiutes to raid neighboring settlements to obtain cattle, a punishing raid by white settlers resulted in the death of scores of old men, women and children.

One of the children killed in the assault was the younger brother of Sarah Winnemulla ("Shell Flower"). The embittered young woman decided that the time had come to fight the white man on his own turf, with his own weapons.

She took to the lecture platform before white audiences, making blistering attacks against the incompetent management of her reservation by corrupt Indian agents. Sarah Winnemulla painted vivid verbal pictures of the suffering and privations of the Paiutes, and she called upon her listeners to force *their* government to deal fairly with *her* people.

They did; and Congress soon enacted special legislation to aid the Paiute Indians.

When John Muir graduated from the University of Wisconsin, he set out to explore the United States on foot. Muir walked the entire distance from Indiana to the Gulf of Mexico, keeping a daily journal in which he entered observations about nature he made along the journey.

Muir proceeded to California, arriving there in 1868. He lived for two years in Yosemite Valley, where he made detailed studies of the landscape and natural growth. He reached the conclusion, contrary to accepted scientific thinking, that Yosemite Valley had been created by glacial action rather than ordinary erosion.

John Muir then headed for Alaska to study glaciers and the indigenous surrounding flora, particularly pines and sequoias.

After his return to California he became distressed by the devastation caused in Yosemite Valley by the overgrazing by large numbers of sheep (he referred to them as "hoofed locusts"). Muir decided to fight.

He invited Robert Underwood Johnson, the editor of *Century* magazine, an influential opinion journal of the day, on a camping trip in Yosemite. When Johnson saw the damage being done by the sheep, he suggested to Muir that the two of them undertake a campaign to have the Yosemite Valley established as a national park.

Muir wrote a series of articles for *Century*, which began to build up public-opinion support for a park. Within a year, Congress not only passed a bill to establish Yosemite National Park, but also gave authority to the President to establish a system of forest reserves.

The Forestry Commission recommended setting aside thirteen forest reserves, totaling over twenty million acres, which were accordingly designated by President Grover Cleveland. Logging interests, caught napping, launched a vigorous lobbying campaign in Congress to undo the President's action. The forest-reserve program was soon in real jeopardy.

John Muir led the counterattack with articles in *Harper's Weekly* and the *Atlantic Monthly,* identifying greed and ignorance as the enemies of the nation's natural resources, and invoking the sacred duty of using natural resources prudently so they could be passed on to future generations in their full richness and beauty. Muir's appeals were the primary factors in halting the repeal movement in Congress and in saving the forest-reserve program.

John Muir was established now in the public mind as a leading champion of the country's natural resources. When President Theodore Roosevelt went on an exploratory camping trip in the West in the spring of 1903, he made it a point to meet with him. Muir cast formal protocol aside and took the President on a hike, urging TR to increase the number of forest preserves and national parks. Muir's arguments hit the mark, and before Roosevelt left office he designated almost 150 million additional acres of forest preserves and sixteen national monuments, and doubled the number of national parks.

Not all John Muir's battles were so successful. When he was an undergraduate at Wisconsin, he set about reforming bad study habits by devising a contraption made of wooden wheels and pulleys that would enforce a regular study schedule. The Muir machine automatically presented the student with the textbook for each current homework assignment for a preset number of minutes, then removed the book and replaced it with another for the proper period of study, and so on. The problem was that the inventor never figured out how to make the student concentrate on his homework instead of daydreaming.

Today "Muir's Folly" can be seen gathering dust in a glass case in the science museum on the university campus at Madison. Fortunately, university students there and elsewhere continue to daydream, as Muir did, of beauty, wilderness and of a better world they will fight to create.

Fighting is an effective reform tool. It generates press and community interest, and often helps to exert pressure on the opposition to do the right thing.

Some well-intentioned do-gooders have a tendency to be excessively polite and to try to avoid controversy. They usually are ineffective.

Controversy is the heart of effective reform. The secret is not to be habitually cantankerous, but to show a fist whenever confronted by selfish, mindless or unfair action.

Special interests and tired politicians usually have much more respect for someone who is ready to fight for what he or she believes is right than for a stuffed-shirt delegation or a written appeal. They are also ready that much sooner to listen to reason. Polite arguments are quickly forgotten, while a verbal punch in the nose may well be a sample of more to come.

Few of us have the opportunity to engage in glorious battles on a grand scale, but we all have opportunities to fight injustice and other wrongs almost every day. Although it is not possible to take up the cudgels every time we see some small wrong, there are occasions when we simply cannot—and must not—turn our backs on injustice and walk away. Vow never to pass up such a challenge when it comes your way. Be ready to fight for your beliefs.

Use the Political Process

Bad officials are elected by good citizens who do
not vote.

—Edmund Burke

In your hands your vote is your machete. You
must not throw it away.

—Luis Muñoz Marin

Norman Thomas was a minister before he became a
radical. Born in Marion, Ohio, where his father was the
Presbyterian pastor, young Thomas earned money de-
livering newspapers while attending public schools.
Later he entered Princeton University with financial
aid from an uncle, and graduated in 1905 as class vale-
dictorian. Then after graduating from divinity school,
Thomas worked in slum parishes, where he became an-
gered by the economic injustice he observed at every
hand.

When the United States entered World War I, the

young idealist abandoned the clergy for politics. Opposing war and the excesses of capitalism, the Socialist party appeared to offer him the best opportunity to speak out against the things he believed were wrong.

Norman Thomas soon saw the opportunities that running for public office afforded him to educate voters and other candidates. Well aware that his chances of ever being elected were remote, Thomas nonetheless became an inveterate candidate—two races for mayor of New York City; two races for governor of New York State; six races for President of the United States—all on the Socialist party ticket.

Thomas ran each race with equal vigor and conviction, traveling thousands of miles, usually in an upper berth to conserve campaign funds, and developing a speaking style that was magnetic and powerful. He was a fierce opponent of both communism and fascism whose goal was a socialist society in which every person had an equal part. He spent a lifetime hammering away at every audience that would listen.

Was the exercise wasted effort? Hardly. Although he lost the elections, Thomas made steady advances for the ideas he espoused. He was one of the first spokesmen for the five-day workweek, unemployment insurance, old-age pensions, minimum-wage laws, abolition of child labor, health insurance for older citizens, public employment agencies, slum clearance, public-works projects, and low-cost housing. These once-radical programs have since become commonplace in our national life. Their early espousal by Norman Thomas helped set the stage for their adoption.

As Thomas grew older, more and more younger Americans identified with his views. When he condemned the Vietnam War as "an immoral war ethically and a stupid war politically," he spoke for millions of young Americans. Thomas was one of the first public figures to oppose the use of atomic bombs. He publicly denounced the bombing of Hiroshima and Nagasaki in 1945, and continued to speak out forcefully for world nuclear disarmament until the end of his life in 1968, years before such sentiments became a popular rallying cry.

Norman Thomas never let a hint of bitterness enter into his campaign speaking. H. L. Mencken, who heard him deliver a campaign address during the 1948 presidential race, described it with unmasked admiration:

> It was full of adept and memorable phrases, some of them apparently almost new. It shined with wit and humor. The speaker poked gentle but devastating fun at all the clowns in the political circus, by no means forgetting himself. There was not a trace of rancor in his speech, and not a trace of Messianic bombast.

The consistent thread through all Norman Thomas's speaking and writing was his abiding respect for individual rights. He fought government loyalty oaths and McCarthyism. He defied a ban against his speaking by Jersey City's Boss Hague and appeared at a rally in that city, even though he was pelted by rotten vegetables. He understood that his role as an articulate opponent was most valuable when it brought about a reexamination of positions and policies he believed were wrong. His long-term record of positive results was impressive, and the example he set of constructive dissent was a high mark for others to follow. As he explained it:

> The secret of a good life is to have the right loyalties and to hold them in the right scale of values. The

value of dissent and dissenters is to make us reappraise those values with supreme concern for truth. Rebellion per se is not a virtue.

One of the most remarkable public servants in modern times was Stanley M. Isaacs of New York City. A lifelong civic leader as well as "politician," he was for many years the sole Republican member of the New York City Council. He was dedicated to social progress and honest government, and was treated with respect and trust by all his colleagues.

Stanley Isaacs was the grandson of a rabbi and the son of a staunch believer in the work of settlement houses. Isaacs himself had taken an early interest in trying to eliminate the worst conditions in the city's slums; and he became an active supporter and advocate for the enactment of a new multiple-dwelling law that set stricter sanitary and safety standards.

Isaacs first ran for office following the Jimmy Walker scandals, when he joined the Fusion ticket headed by Fiorello H. La Guardia and ran for borough president of Manhattan.

As soon as he took office, Isaacs cleaned out the political hangers-on on the borough president's staff, destroying all hope for regular organizational support for renomination to the post. So he ran instead for the city council on the Independent ticket, and was elected on the strength of popular support for his reform work.

Stanley Isaacs became an urban folk hero as a member of the city council, where, as the only member of an opposition party, he repeatedly and vocally opposed waste and poor budget planning. Unlike other politicians, he had no illusions about the risks he was taking by being outspoken. Good government was his objective, not winning reelection. He summed it up:

> Our job is to fight for what we believe in, win when we can, and if we are beaten, from time to time, start right over again; and not to retreat or to sulk.

Running for office to espouse a cause need not always lead to political obscurity. In one case at least, it had the reverse effect and changed a political has-been into a successful candidate for President of the United States.

When Abraham Lincoln ran for office, he was frankly motivated by personal ambition and the desire to make a name for himself. In 1834, Lincoln managed to be elected to the Illinois state legislature, where he served four successive terms. Then he ran successfully for the United States House of Representatives in 1846. His service in the House was disillusioning, and he was notable only for his obscurity. Lincoln opposed the Mexican-American War on moral grounds, thereby alienating his home constituency and forfeiting any chance he had to run for reelection.

The end of his service in the House in 1849 appeared to be the end of Lincoln's political career. He settled down to the full-time practice of law in Springfield. Then something happened which so aroused Lincoln that he decided to return to politics to fight for a principle.

That something was the passage of the Kansas-Nebraska Act, sponsored by Illinois Senator Stephen A. Douglas, which directly repudiated the Missouri Compromise and allowed slavery to be extended into the Northwest. Lincoln was outraged. For him this action

by Congress was a total repudiation of a national ideal.
"If slavery is not wrong, nothing is wrong," he said.

But the path was not easy. He ran for the Illinois
state legislature on an antislavery platform—and lost.

Lincoln sought the Whig nomination for the
United States Senate—and lost again.

In 1856 Lincoln joined the Republican party and
sought nomination as Vice-President—but failed once
more.

Finally in 1858 he found the opportunity to use
his political candidacy to espouse the antislavery
cause. Lincoln received the Republican nomination for
United States Senator from Illinois to oppose the Democratic incumbent, Stephen Douglas. Douglas accepted
Lincoln's challenge to a series of debates, and the two
candidates confronted each other in seven debates
around the state which have become legendary. Lincoln presented his arguments with skill, and the press
was rhapsodic. But not the electorate. Lincoln lost
again.

Finally, in February 1860 Lincoln was invited to
address an antislavery meeting in the Great Hall of
Cooper Union in New York City. He labored over his
speech, which electrified a sophisticated audience assembled by William Cullen Bryant to hear him. He
told his listeners that there was little hope of eliminating slavery from the states where it now existed, that
the real challenge was to prevent its spread into the
territories. He urged them not to grope for "some mid-
dle ground between the right and the wrong":

> Neither let us be slandered from our duty by false
> accusations against us, nor frightened from it by men-
> aces of destruction to the government, not of dungeons

to ourselves. Let us have faith that right makes might, and in that faith let us to the end dare do our duty as we understand it.

At the Republican convention in Chicago in May 1860, Abraham Lincoln succeeded in winning nomination as a compromise candidate on the third ballot over militant abolitionist William H. Seward. The election campaign itself was a three-way race, giving Lincoln at last the opportunity to be elected to office, despite the fact that he failed to win a majority of the popular vote. He had won in spite of his cause.

Citizen activism is the more usual course for advancing a cause in the political arena, and the most consistent advocate of good government in United States political history has been the League of Women Voters.

The League was organized by leaders of the women's rights movement at the conclusion of the successful drive to win women's suffrage. The 1919 annual convention of the National American Woman Suffrage Association authorized each state in which women's suffrage had been adopted to establish a League of Women Voters as an auxiliary. One of the first state Leagues was created in New York, with its organizing meeting held in Utica in November 1919. Narcissa Cox Vanderlip was elected as the New York State League's first chairman.

A handsome and highly intelligent woman of thirty-nine, Mrs. Vanderlip was the mother of six children, and the wife of the millionaire chairman of the country's largest private bank, the National City Bank. She had the resources and ability needed to whip the new citizen organization into a fighting machine, and she did just that, traveling from county to county to organize local chapters and stir them into a frenzy of enthusiasm for using the women's vote as a positive force for good. Early objectives adopted by the New York State League were health insurance for workers, an eight-hour workday, and a minimum-wage law. The League also took on formidable opponents, the first being United States Senator James W. Wadsworth, a Republican from Geneseo, New York, who had been a vitriolic opponent of women's suffrage as well as of the League of Nations.

Mrs. Vanderlip, herself a Republican, was outspoken in her attacks on Wadsworth as "obsolete, a thing of the past":

> He is an old-fashioned machine-made article. He represents only the inside regulars of his party. It is our duty to see that the next Senator represents the ideals of our citizens.

Wadsworth handily won reelection, but he ran 800,000 votes behind the head of the ticket (Warren G. Harding), a fact that was not lost on the party regulars. Organized good-government voters could do serious damage when they put their minds to it. (The League of Women Voters has since adopted a policy of not opposing or supporting individual candidates.)

Throughout its sixty-year history, the League has steadily supported public-interest objectives, and has had a significant impact on legislation in both the state and the nation's capitals.

The typical citizen foray into politics is to achieve a single objective, like public health or safety.

Mary Eliza McDowell, daughter of a steel-mill owner in Chicago, grew up in wealthy suburbs and dabbled in church, temperance and social work. When she was forty, a group of faculty members at the University of Chicago asked her to organize a settlement house to serve as a social-service laboratory in the immigrant neighborhood behind the Chicago stockyards. Ms. McDowell moved into a small second-floor-rear apartment in a tenement building in the area, and set out to win acceptance from the families of the stockyard workers of Irish, German, Polish, Lithuanian, Bohemian and Slavic background who were her neighbors.

Ms. McDowell's tiny day-care nursery soon added classes in English and summer outings to city parks, and eventually a neighborhood playground and a gymnasium were constructed. The area consisted of unpaved streets with rows of frame houses; the air was permeated with the heavy stench of the slaughterhouses, the city garbage dump, and Bubbly Creek, a segment of the Chicago River choked with fermenting raw sewage. The community had the worst health record in the entire city, and Mary McDowell decided to do something about it.

Her approach was to become actively engaged in area politics. She organized workers at every local election. She ran as a candidate for the county legislature. Then she set about recruiting well-to-do members of the Chicago Women's City Club to educate press and public about the conditions of the garbage dump and open sewer. Ms. McDowell went on fact-finding trips around the United States and in Europe to learn different techniques for the proper handling of garbage. Armed with facts and well-placed supporters, she then laid

siege to the Chicago City Council. The council finally
responded to the demands of the "Garbage Lady" and
in 1913 voted funds to replace the open dump with
garbage-reduction plants, to fill in Bubbly Creek and
to construct a new sewer.

Ms. McDowell eventually became prominent in
the women's suffrage movement and in organizations
dedicated to improving race relations, but nothing
proved to be more gratifying than her use of the political process to force the Chicago City Council to improve conditions for the families who lived behind the
stockyards.

In 1899, a devastating fire, caused by careless lumbering practices, destroyed a ranch and a stand of
giant redwoods in the Santa Cruz Mountains of California. Josephine Clifford McCrackin, a minor author
married to the wealthy mineowner who owned the
ranch, was outraged by the mindless and unnecessary
destruction of natural resources. She wrote an article
attacking the lumbering interests for their indifference to preservation of natural resources and wildlife.
The article, which appeared in the *Santa Cruz Sentinel*
in March 1900, was reprinted widely. Women's clubs,
San Francisco officials and concerned citizens organized a crusading committee to save the redwoods, with
Mrs. McCrackin elected as one of the first officers. The
Save-the-Redwoods League organized an intensive lobbying campaign, which resulted in the state purchas-
ing 3800 acres of redwood forest in the Big Basin
region, and in the creation of Redwood National Park,
one of the finest remaining stands of redwood in the
United States.

* * *

Dr. Rosa Gantt, an eye, ear, nose and throat specialist
in Spartanburg, South Carolina, daughter of a leading
Jewish merchant in Charleston, was one of the first
women to graduate from the Medical College of South
Carolina. She had received graduate training at New
York University before entering into practice in her
home state. Deeply aware of the medical needs of the
Southeast, Dr. Gantt organized fellow professionals in
her state to push for regular medical checkups for
schoolchildren. When she managed to get the law
through the South Carolina legislature, the governor
vetoed it, dismissing Dr. Gantt as a "crank." She did
not give up. Eventually the measure was passed and
signed into law in 1920.

Dr. Gantt also led direct public-education programs, particularly in the back country, to warn
householders about the sanitary problems associated
with house flies, rats and common drinking cups. She
helped start a program in the southern Appalachians
to combat pellagra; and was responsible for the establishment of maternity shelters, health houses and
clinics throughout the region.

Not every political achievement requires the passage of
legislation. Sometimes a single symbolic act can
change the direction of governmental policy—a public
statement by a chief executive, attending an event,
making a tour of inspection, a major speech, a public
appearance, a letter. Frequently a simple step, easily
taken, can have a major impact.

Theodore Roosevelt made a major contribution to
improved racial understanding when he invited

Booker T. Washington to come to dinner at the White House in 1901. Washington was the first black ever to be received and entertained as a guest in the President's house. The symbolic act electrified the nation. Senators made fiery speeches. Newspapers published editorials. People talked.

An ex-slave, Booker T. Washington had worked his way through Hampton Institute and become a schoolteacher; in 1881 he agreed to head up a brand-new normal school for blacks in Alabama. Under his direction, Tuskegee Institute grew from a henhouse to an educational facility of over 100 buildings on 30,000 acres of land, teaching 38 trades and professions to black youngsters to open up opportunities for self-sufficiency. Inviting him to dinner at the White House contributed to the stature and growth of Tuskegee, and to the larger cause of expanded educational opportunities for minorities.

Theodore Roosevelt made a symbolic contribution to government support for the arts by appointing Edwin Arlington Robinson a special agent in the New York Customhouse when he learned that the young poet was unemployed and penniless. Roosevelt's instructions to Robinson upon his appointment contained the essence of practical patronage:

> I want you to understand that I expect you to think poetry first and Customs second.

All our lives are governed to a large degree by the policies of government—local, state and federal. "Politics" is the method by which we affect those policies—by running for office, by lobbying activities, by grass-roots politicking, and by generating public- or private-opinion pressure on officeholders. The object of all these techniques is to persuade (or force) officials to look out for the public interest.

What motivates a person in public office to move in one direction rather than another?

Friendship
Reciprocity
Anger
Fear of Political Reprisal
Expectation of Reward
Flattery
Avoidance of Public Criticism

Overriding all, the public official is governed by the desire for reelection or promotion. It is a standing joke in Washington that if you were to call out, "Mr. President!" in the Senate chamber, a hundred heads would look up.

How can we put these factors to work in support of our own cause?

Friendship. Support a candidate for public office at the earliest possible moment. Be generous with your time and money. Volunteer to do the unpleasant tasks that are most needed—like raising campaign funds or arranging for endorsements. An official's closest friends are invariably those who were on hand to help when the going was toughest.

Reciprocity. Get someone to request a public official to take a particular stand or action who is in a position to return the favor—it could be another official or a major contributor. "One hand washes the other."

Anger. Encourage a political opponent or a jour-

nalist to criticize the official for inaction or heartless-
ness on the critical issue. Get that individual in an "I'll
show you" frame of mind.

Fear of Political Reprisal. Line up civic leaders
and organizations from the official's home district in
support of your position, so that he must risk their dis-
favor and possible opposition next election if he moves
in the wrong direction.

Expectation of Reward. Invite the official to speak
before an audience known to favor your position. Present him with a distinguished-service award. Arrange
for press coverage.

Flattery. Have celebrities write to the official or
make personal calls. Invite him to a private function in
an exclusive setting.

Avoidance of Public Criticism. Try to persuade
editorial writers in the local press to support your position and to question the official's inaction. Persuade
the most likely opponent of the incumbent to support
your stand. Write a "Letter to the Editor" urging the
official to do the right thing.

This is not an exhaustive list by any means, but it does
provide a series of practical examples of how citizens
can influence public officials to act in a particular way.

The most important fact to remember is that the
dominant motivating force in any public official's
mind is the need *to be reelected or to be promoted to a
higher position.* Once this principle is understood, you
have the secret for getting results. Everything you do
should convey the clear meaning that adopting your
position will aid the official's reelection or promotion,
and not doing so will have the reverse effect.

How you use the political process is up to you. Running hopeless races as Norman Thomas did gives you a powerful podium. Most political adversaries try to minimize differences with their opponents on issues they do not particularly care about, in order to reduce the possibility of negative impact on voters. Therefore, if you, the underdog, espouse a particular position loud and long enough, the chances are that some journalist or voter will ask your opponent his position on the same issue, and, lo and behold, he will *agree* with you! When you follow up after election with some of the techniques suggested above, it will give you a big headstart.

The important thing is to become involved in the political process at some point if you really want to achieve results.

Politics is a serious business, but most citizen politicians make the fatal mistake of dealing with other politicians with a tiresome earnestness that is self-defeating. Politicians are gregarious—they have to be to win votes—and they respond best to friendliness and goodwill, kept within proper bounds. Above all, they appreciate good humor and good sportsmanship. The civic activist who gets off a funny line is likely to be remembered long after the one with a long face.

The most popular figures in American political history have usually been those with a sense of humor.

Compare Adlai Stevenson with Richard Nixon.

When Adlai Stevenson lost his first bid for the presidency in 1952, he told his disappointed supporters on election night:

Someone asked me, as I came in, down on the street, how I felt, and I was reminded of a story that a fellow-townsman of ours used to tell, Abraham Lincoln. They asked him how he felt once after an unsuccessful election. He said he felt like a little boy who had stubbed his toe in the dark. He said that he was to old to cry, but it hurt too much to laugh.

In 1956, when Stevenson again lost the presidency, he told his assembled supporters:

Be of good cheer. And remember, my dear friends, what a wise man said—"A merry heart doeth good like a medicine, but a broken spirit dryeth the bones."

In marked contrast, when Richard Nixon lost his bid for the governorship of California in 1962, he held a press conference the following day in which he made a rambling series of charges that the press had unfairly reported his campaign. His statement ended with bitterness and resentment:

You won't have Nixon to kick around any more, because gentlemen, this is my last press conference. . . .

A sense of humor is particularly effective at times of public trial and stress. In March 1981, on the day after he had been struck down by a would-be assassin's bullet, President Ronald Reagan cheered millions of Americans by making lighthearted wisecracks about his situation. After leaving the operating table where the bullet was removed from his lung, with tubes in his throat preventing him from speaking, the President wrote the following note to his aides:

Winston Churchill said, "There is no more exhilarating feeling than being shot without result."

A short while later the President wrote this note:

> If I had this much attention in Hollywood, I would never have left.

One of the masters in the use of humor in his public appearances was President John F. Kennedy. Theodore Sorensen, his speech-writing aide during those years, described Kennedy's approach to platform humor in his lively biography:

> He believed topical, tasteful, pertinent, pointed humor at the beginning of his remarks to be a major means of establishing audience rapport; and he would work with me as diligently for the right opening witticism, or take as much pride the next day in some spontaneous barb he had flung, as he would on the more substantive paragraphs in his text.

Kennedy and Sorensen were always on the alert for new material. When they heard good stories told successfully by a toastmaster or another speaker, they would jot them down. They scanned newspaper columns and other writings for humorous quotes, particularly those dealing with history and government. Finley Peter Dunne and Will Rogers were favorite sources:

> No laugh-getter once used or even considered was ever discarded. A large "humor folder" in my files grew continuously. Omitting all anecdotes from the texts that were distributed to the press usually avoided their being publicized, and thus made possible their use in another speech in another part of the country. Audiences watching him scribbling away during dinner often thought he was rewriting his speech, as at times he was. More often he was jotting down the open-

ing lines most appropriate to that audience, working in many cases from a typewritten "humor list" of one-line reminders.

Kennedy's rules were never to use off-color remarks in public, and to avoid any ethnic references except for jokes about the political liabilities of his own religion. He particularly enjoyed poking fun at himself, but was careful to avoid humor that might sound bitter or cause injury to others.

Abraham Lincoln, however, was probably the President most remembered for his droll stories.

He had used humor extensively in his legal practice, in addressing juries and judges and engaging in banter with other lawyers. When he traveled on circuit from town to town to attend court sessions, Lincoln often spent his spare time reading *Joe Miller's Joke Book* (originally published in 1739!), adapting the stories to fit the local scene.

Lincoln had also used humor effectively on the campaign trail.

During the course of his debates with Stephen A. Douglas in the summer of 1858, as Douglas became more and more aggressive in his attacks on his opponent, Lincoln responded with a light touch of good humor. On one occasion, Douglas wound up his remarks with a bitter attack on Lincoln's career, saying that Lincoln had tried everything and had always been a failure:

He had tried farming and failed at that, had tried flatboating and failed at that, had tried schoolteaching and failed at that, had sold liquor in a saloon and failed at that, had tried law and failed at that, and now he had gone into politics and was doomed to make the worst failure of all.

Lincoln sat there chuckling. Then he rose and thanked Senator Douglas for his summary of Lincoln's career, which he said was all true:

> I have worked on a farm; I have split rails; I have worked on a flatboat; I have tried to practice law. There is just one thing that Judge Douglas forgot to relate. He says that I sold liquor over a counter. He forgot to tell you that, while I was on one side of the counter, the Judge was always on the other side.

Use these lessons well, and in good humor, and you, too, can make a difference.

How to Enrich Your Own Life

On the day in 1933 when Franklin Delano Roosevelt was inaugurated President of the United States, he paid a courtesy call on former Justice Oliver Wendell Holmes. Holmes was then ninety-two years old. The President found him in his library reading Plato.

After an exchange of greetings, Roosevelt asked, "Why do you read Plato, Mr. Justice?"

The response was unhesitating: "To improve my mind, Mr. President."

Improving one's mind is not only good for Supreme Court justices, it is a hallmark of almost every man and woman of accomplishment.

General of the Army George C. Marshall had a thirst for local history. On every new assignment or trip, he searched out the specific places connected with the history of the area—ancient roads in the Philip-

pines, battlefields in Manchuria, the site of Joan of
Arc's baptism, the remains of old Fort Vancouver.
Marshall also read extensively in biography and his-
tory, but also found time to read Western novels.

When Winston Churchill was graduated from the
Royal Military Academy at Sandhurst, he was com-
missioned a second lieutenant in a cavalry regiment
and sent off to India. While there, he began to realize
that his military-school education had left him unlet-
tered in literature and history. He decided to teach
himself and began by reading Gibbon's *History of the
Decline and Fall of the Roman Empire,* all eight volumes. There followed one classic after another. He
spent time reading books of quotations, for he said
later:

> It is a good thing for an uneducated man to read
> books of quotations. *Bartlett's Familiar Quotations* is
> an admirable work, and I studied it intently. The quo-
> tations when engraved upon the memory give you good
> thoughts. They also make you anxious to read the au-
> thors and look for more.

General Dwight D. Eisenhower was a bird-watcher by
avocation. When he first landed in Italy, he asked his
brother to send him a handbook on Italian birds.

Bird-watching has an appeal for people in many
different walks of life. Financial expert Guy Emerson
used to arrange his business trips so they would coin-
cide with the best time for observing warblers, shore
birds and ducks.

Crawford H. Greenewalt, president of E. I. du
Pont de Nemours and Company for many years, had
the unusual hobby of photographing hummingbirds in

flight. The result was a 1960 book of photographs of hummingbirds in all parts of the world. Over the course of seven years, Mr. Greenewalt found time on weekends and vacations to travel over 100,000 miles tracking down the most exotic hummingbird species in North and South America, finally producing the first comprehensive portfolio of color photographs ever published. The combination of his executive knowledge and avocational interest produced a work hailed by the curator of birds of the American Museum of Natural History as an important scientific contribution:

> Mr. Greenewalt has brought to his study the enthusiasm and the organizing capacity which have made him one of America's top industrial executives. Characteristically, he has combined sound and imaginative scholarship with advanced technological methods to reach new and exciting conclusions.

In some cases, outside interests have led to second careers. Charles Broley, who retired from his position as a bank manager in Canada at the age of sixty, stopped off to have lunch with the head of the Audubon Society, Richard Pough, on his way to Florida. Pough suggested to Broley, almost as an aside, that he consider banding Florida bald eagles. The retired banker seized on the idea, and for the next ten years tracked down nesting bald eagles in their aeries throughout southern Florida. Before he began his banding activities, only 166 bald eagles had ever been marked; Broley banded more than a thousand over a ten-year period. The result was a much broader knowledge of the life-styles and habits of the eagle, contrib-

uting to new ideas on how to save the bird when the
population was threatened because of the growing use
of pesticides.

Reading newspaper obituaries often gives a
glimpse of the wide range of outside interests and activities cultivated by men and women of accomplishment. From his obituary one learned, for example, that
Edward Steichen, the pioneering photographer who organized the Family of Man exhibition at the Museum
of Modern Art, had a lifelong interest in botany, and
had gained recognition for his work in crossbreeding
several new species of flowers.

Thomas Jefferson was remarkable for the restlessness
of his mind, which was rarely idle. Even during his retirement from public life after he left the presidency,
Jefferson kept up a heavy schedule of letter writing
(which resulted in a gold mine of research material)
and worked hard at improving public education in his
home state of Virginia. ("Enlighten the people generally," he wrote in 1816, "and tyranny and oppres-
sions of both mind and body will vanish like evil spirits
at the dawn of day.") During his lifetime, Jefferson
pioneered in research in many scientific fields: botany,
ethnology, geography, paleontology. He was an inventor, an architect and a student of history. He could
read five languages: French, Italian, Spanish, Greek
and Latin; and he compiled such an extensive personal
library (ten thousand volumes) that it was purchased
as the nucleus of the Library of Congress after the
burning of Washington in the War of 1812.

Jefferson was also a patron of the arts and owned
one of the best private collections of paintings and

sculpture in the United Sates. When he was at home, he managed a large farm and sponsored numerous creative projects, including an excellent vineyard and a nail factory. Jefferson's secret of keeping his mind active and alert was to exercise every part of it—continuously.

Gene Tunney, former heavyweight champion of the world, discovered Shakespeare when he was a soldier in World War I. Tunney tackled *A Winter's Tale,* one of Shakespeare's less successful efforts, and read it through not once but *ten* times. Then he went on to other Shakespeare plays.

In his autobiography William Lyon Phelps of Yale University described a discussion he had with Tunney about the importance of having outside interests:

> He regarded it as fortunate that he loved good books and music, etc., quite apart from the intrinsic value of such things; because, during his weeks of active training, he could at any moment divert his mind by reading a good book or listening to the piano. It is not healthy for any man or woman to be obsessed by one thought; the mind becomes hagridden, and the nerves go to pieces. The brain needs variety; thus the more avocations a man has outside of his work, the more efficiently he will do that work, and the fresher and healthier his mind will be.

Professor Phelps invited the heavyweight champion to New Haven to address a Shakespeare class. Tunney arrived on April 23, 1928, to find a large auditorium jammed with curious students and onlookers:

He told the students they had had every educational advantage and he had had none. "But when you are graduated and out in the world, then your case will be like mine. Your professors will not be able to help you; you will have to do it all for yourself. If you succeed, it will be because you have had the necessary will-power and perseverance."

Henry L. Stimson, the New York lawyer who rendered extraordinary public service as Secretary of War during World War II—and who inaugurated merit selection of assistants and nonpolitical administration of the United States Attorney's office for the Southern District of New York when he was appointed by President Theodore Roosevelt—made it a practice to spend part of each summer in the West. Like many other people who have come to know and love nature, Stimson drew energy and relaxation from his explorations. He saw the West when it was still part of the frontier. He visited with the Indians and helped map portions of Montana which now include Glacier National Park. After his marriage, Stimson's wife shared his enthusiasm for the wilderness and joined him on his summer trips.

In his biography, written at the end of his life with the help of McGeorge Bundy, Stimson explained the impact of these out-of-door expeditions:

Looking back, I find it hard to exaggerate the effect of these experiences on my later life. That effect, physical, mental, and moral, was great. Not only is self-confidence gained by such a life, but ethical principles tend to become simpler by the impact of the wilderness and by contact with the men who live in it. Moral problems are divested of the confusion and complications which civilization throws around them. Self-ishness cannot be easily concealed, and the importance of courage, truthfulness, and frankness is increased. To a certain extent the effect is similar to the code of honor learned by the soldier in the field.

Justice Louis D. Brandeis understood the importance of change of pace and change of activity. He, too, spent summer vacations hiking in the wilderness, or canoe-ing, or sailing. No matter how busy he was, he always took off the full month of August to catch up on his reading and to enjoy the outdoors. "I soon learned that I could do twelve months' work in eleven months, but not in twelve," he said. "The bow must be strung and unstrung."

Few things are more disheartening than encountering people who say they have "nothing to do" and are bored by inactivity. The real problem in life is not that there is nothing to do, but that there is too much to do and so little time in which to do it. The essential ingre-dient of a full life is an active mind bursting with in-terests. Two or three levels of active interests can always be pursued simultaneously—one concerned with making a living; a second, with accomplishing something in the public interest; the third, simply with the pleasure of learning.

Public Service Checklist

In the unlikely event that any reader has reached this point without having several areas of possible public-service activity in mind, a random checklist is included for brainstorming purposes. It is not intended to be comprehensive, but instead is designed as a pump primer to get your thought processes moving.

Opportunities for public service are virtually everywhere. The key to choosing the right one for you is *not* to look for existing organizations and simply sign up with one (although such organizations obviously deserve your support). Instead, search for a cause which arouses your sense of right and wrong. Preferably you should look for a cause that has been neglected, where little or nothing is being done—one you can identify with and in which you can measure your own achievements.

When you have made your choice, get started right away. Even if it is only to research the facts, get involved. Do not procrastinate. Do it now.

Start making a difference.

Potential Areas of Public Service

Public education
Public libraries
Literacy training
Freedom of speech and/or press
Freedom of religion
Health care
Housing
Child care
Family support
Community services
Recreation
Citizen participation in politics
Job training
Job placement
Small-business opportunities
Public safety
Law enforcement
Court system
Corrections
Prisoner rehabilitation
Senior-citizen care
Group cultural heritage
Performing arts
Graphic and fine arts
Literature
Natural resources—wilderness areas
Birds and animals
Architectural quality
Historic sites and landmarks

Your approach to each item on the above list should be to examine it thoroughly with your mind's eye, asking such questions as:

1. Does this area need to be protected, improved, expanded?
2. Does it need to be overhauled?
3. Should there be greater access for more people?

When you settle on one (or two or three) areas that challenge you emotionally and intellectually, go to work to find out everything you can about needs and solutions. Develop your own action plan for achieving the results you want (following role models you have read about in this book).

Begin exerting leadership—quietly or aggressively—even if you are only leading yourself.

Review your progress from time to time. Find out where you are wasting time and where you are moving forward. Stop doing the former and do more of the latter.

Gather supporters as you move along, but be sure they will really help your advance.

Above all, commit your heart, your mind and all your energy to your cause—and you cannot fail to make a difference.

Index

About the Author

Whitney North Seymour, Jr., was brought up in a family deeply involved in community and professional service. His father was president of the American Bar Association and the New York Legal Aid Society; an officer of many other legal organizations; a pioneer leader in landmarks preservation; and Assistant Solicitor General of the United States, in addition to being a senior partner in a large New York law firm that produced two United States Senators, a Secretary of State and other public servants. He was active in church, alumni and community work.

Mr. Seymour himself has served as a New York state senator and as United States Attorney for the Southern District of New York. He has been an officer and director in civic and philanthropic organizations concerned with housing, recreation, the arts, historic preservation and public libraries; he has served as president of the New York State Bar Association and in executive positions in many other professional groups. Mr. Seymour was a co-founder of the Natural Resources Defense Council; and has served as *pro bono* counsel in many legal cases.

The author and his wife, Catryna, and their two

daughters have worked together in causes varying from litter control to political reform. Together they founded and jointly operate an independent publishing firm that emphasizes the book arts and the American literary tradition.

He is a graduate of Princeton University (1947) and Yale Law School (1950), and served in the U.S. Army for three and a half years during World War II (two years in the Pacific), rising from the rank of private to captain.